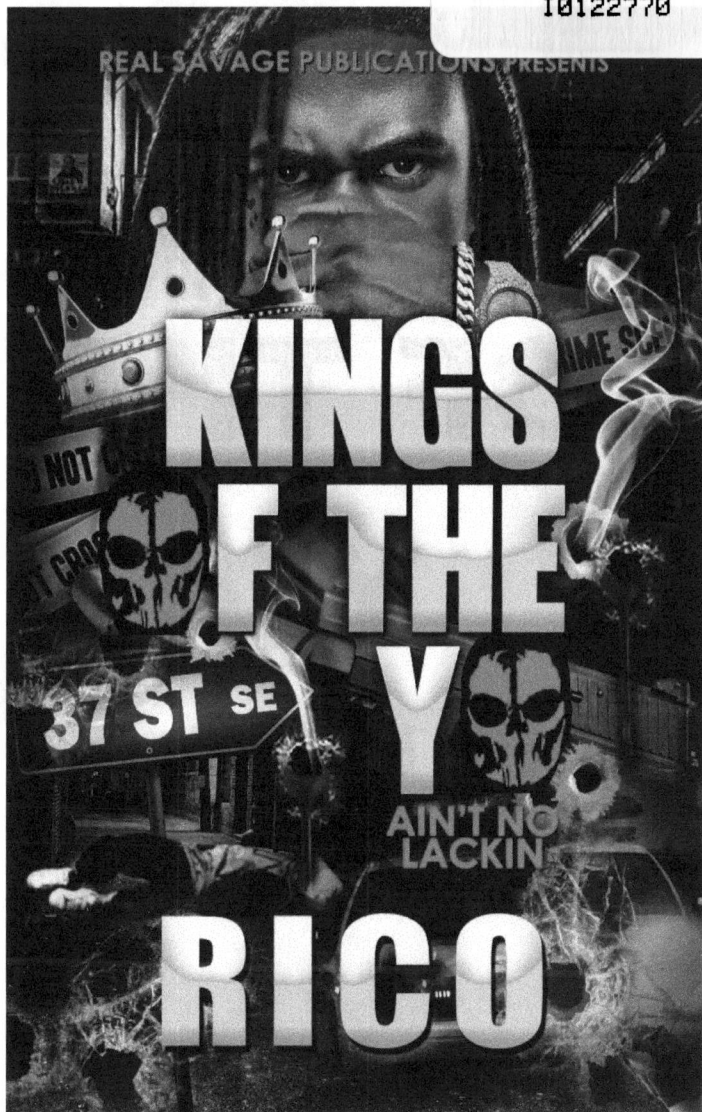

KINGS

OF THE

YO

AIN'T NO LACKIN

RICO

REAL SAVAGE

PRODUCTIONS

ACKNOWLEDGEMENTS

First off, I want to give thanks and praise to Allah, the most high. Without him, I will not have had the ability to write this book or do anything else without his help and blessings. Secondly, I would like to send my love to my mother, Katina who passed away and is "Isha Allah" in the paradise. Without her, I wouldn't be here. I want to say sorry to you mother for everything that I had never got the chance to say sorry for, and for what my brothers put you through as well.

Allah knows it was too much to bare. The average woman would've crumbled with ease with half of what we put you through, but you stayed strong and tried your best even when 3 of your 4 sons was facing life sentences, and the other one already sentenced to 29 years at just 15 years old (smh). I have so much to say to you, but it's hard to write and would take a whole notebook. I'm just hurt that you didn't get to see my daughter Ma' Ziyah and get to enjoy your 2 granddaughter's (Ma'Ziyah and Kaitlyn). They are so beautiful and smart. I know you would've spoiled them like you did Diamond. Mom, I love you and Miss you more that words could ever say, and I hope to see your beautiful face again.

Now that I got that off my chest, I want to give a special thanks to *Dynasty's Visionary Designs* for editing my book and designing my book cover. I appreciate you and thank you.

Now I want to give a special shout out to both of my grandmother's, Beverly and Amelia. I love y'all more than y'all will ever understand.

To my aunt Leeli who always would ride and die for me and held me down when most counted me out, I love you and thank you for your love and loyalty.

Shout out to my father, Popoo (S.W.). I love you slim. Hopefully that 25 and under Law get you back on the streets so we can finally build a stronger bond and you can be there for your granddaughter's.

I can't forget my two sisters, London and Diamond. I love y'all more than words can describe.

I want to thank my daughter's mother, Celsie. Even though we ain't there (lol), nah, for real though. I want to thank you for giving me a beautiful daughter. In my DJ Khalid voice, *"I'm forever grateful."* LMAO

To my beautiful daughter, Ma' Ziyah. I love you so much princess. You are my heart and the air I breathe. You are the reason I changed in so many ways and now look at life differently. I miss you so much and will be by your side soon to give you the world.

I'm not finished yet, lol.

I want to give a shout out to my Day 1 man and brother, Squirt. He and I were cellmates when I first thought about writing this book. He was going to co-write it with me, but we got split up, so I just kept going by myself. You already know where we stand slim. We brother's and we've been through hell and back together and never folded. Being blood brothers couldn't make us any closer. Even though we only months apart, I remember when you first really jumped off the porch, LLS. I had you doing a lot of wild shit, kill! But we 'bout to get out there soon and fuck them steets up and get rich. I'ma holla at you later tho. Love4Life.

Shout out to my blood brother, Lil E. I love you to death, bra. Keep your head up! When I touch down, if you ain't out there or on your way, I'ma make sure a lawyer on your case night and day until you back out there shining again. You already know you ain't going to need for anything.

Lastly, I'ma shout out the good men I mess with and got much love and respect for. I can't forget about the real, behind the hall.

S/O my nigga Moochie 'CTU'. You already know where we stand Slimmmm! Lol

S/O my niggas Twin Glocks '501'. Free Josh!

S/O my niggas since Day 1, Bow and JJ '37/O St'.

S/O my nigga Brill (Baltimore).

S/O Rocc, Say, and Zo '22nd'. Rocc, what's sup? Big Boy, I told you I was going to finish dis joint!

S/O to my old cellie and my big homie Kevin Gray. I love you slim. Hopefully I get back up on you before I roll in 2022.

S/O to my uncle Chin, Pimp, Birdy, and Draper 'Southwest Kst'. I loved y'all niggas since I was in pampers LMAO!

S/O my niggas Dirty 'Edgewood'. Hit me, you got my info you burnt out ass nigga.

S/O my nigga Fat Face and Phil '1-7 Uptown'.

S/O my nigga B- Love 'KWA'.

S/O to my old head and young niggas from Yo '37th'. June, Pat, L, No Savage, Fat Marcus, my lil cousin Jose, Choo Choo, Drock, Nine, Lil SV, Tony B, KGR (what it do bruh), my nigga Shy, and lil brother Loc. 'LL4L'.

Before I go, let me shout out my good out of town men.

S/O my nigga mass 'Newark'.

S/O big Troy 'Philly'.

S/O CV 'LA'.

S/O Primo 'Tampa'.

S/O Blizz 'Alabama'.

A big S/O to my white boy K. Much Love for typing this joint up for me.

And S/O to all the good men I missed. Y'all know who you are. Get up with me. I should be on the streets in 18 months! For all the real niggas doing time, keep y'all heads up. I'm gone.

In order to be labelled 'KING' you have to have a lion mentality to protect, feed and be willing to die for your's and your family. That's what all of us are willing to do!

Rico

CHAPTER 1

"Where da fuck y'all about to go?" Shitty asked his little brother Loc and his partner in crime KGR.

Shitty is 19yrs old, dark-skinned, 5'8', 140 lbs and skinny with chest-length dreadlocks in his hair. He was probably, perhaps the most cruddy nigga you'd ever meet, but loyal to his crew. His little brother Loc is 15yrs old going on 40, 5'5', 125 lbs, light-brown skinned with dreadlocks that hang just above his navel. Loc got the nickname Loc from the Actor Marlon Wayans in the movie *Don't Be A Menace To South Central While Drinking Juice In The Hood*, his name was *Loc Dog*, and he lives up to his name. KGR is 17yrs old, light-skinned, 5'6", 130 lbs with dreadlocks as long as Loc's. KGR stands for *Can't Get Right*. He just uses the letter *K* because, like I said, he just can't get right. KGR just like Loc didn't care or it just didn't matter to him, he'd do whatever, whenever, to whoever.

"Bra, we 'bout to go find a move!" Loc said excitedly like he was about to hit the lottery.

"*Go find a move?* Either y'all got a move or y'all need to tighten up. Y'all better stop robbing motherfuckers without face masks! Y'all playing a nigga's game to put that bag on y'all heads," Shitty advised Loc and KGR.

RICO | KINGS OF THE YO

"A nigga ain't going to do shit, but get robbed or hit wit' these 30s," Loc said as he and KGR both pulled out a Glock 26 9s with 30s in them.

"Yea, a'ight," Shitty said laughing.

"KGR where your brova at?"

"He right dere," KGR replied, pointing behind Shitty to his brother Squirt who was coming from behind the building with Lil' E.

"We gone bra!" Loc yelled to Shitty before he and KGR started jogging in the opposite direction of Squirt and Lil E.

"Where the fuck dem wild niggas goin' bra?" Squirt said as he and Lil E walked up and gave Shitty dap.

Squirt was KGR's older brother, he is 19yrs old light brown-skinned, 5'9', and chubby weighing 195 lbs with a low haircut, waves, and a Muslim like beard. Squirt was a laid back kind of guy, but at the same time with all the bullshit, if it was beneficial for him, Squirt just like everybody else in his crew had a quick trigger finger. Lil E was Shitty and Loc's other brother, he was two years younger than Shitty and two years older than Loc at 17yrs old. Lil E is brown-skinned, 5'6', 130 lbs with a low haircut. Lil E was laid back for the most part and always smiling for nothing at all, but don't let the smile fool you Lil' E was as ruthless as they come when needed to be.

"I don't know, bra. Dey said dey was 'bout to go find a move. So, you know what dat means dey 'bout to go rob anybody. Dem niggas be lunchin', kid!" Shitty replied to Squirt.

"Well, speaking of a move, I got a move for us," Lil E said.

"Where at Squirt?"

"Down Double R, dem niggas down dere gambling big! Turk called my phone and said dey down dere shooting 50s kill and dey gambling behind the white buildings, lackin'."

"Who all down dere?" Squirt said.

"Turk ain't say it, but shiddd dat shit don't matter who down there. Dem niggas shooting 50s fuck all dem niggas, kid!" Shitty said to Squirt. "Call Turk's phone back and tell him to step off because we about to come down dere and bag them niggas and tell him don't say shit to anybody wit' his 'noid ass, real live," Shitty said to Lil E.

"A'ight," Lil E said to Shitty pulling out his phone to call Turk smiling.

"Turk said he 'bout to step off right now because he just lost what he brought outside!" Lil E yelled.

"So, y'all ready?" Shitty said.

"We gone," Squirt said, whippin' out his black Glock .30.

A few minutes later Shitty, Squirt and Lil E were walking down Ridge Road that everyone calls Double R on the outskirts of 37th Street Southeast (or the yo). As they walk behind the white buildings on the Double R they see Turk walking in the opposite direction and a crowd of eight people standing around shooting dice. Amongst the eight people gambling was White Timmy, Blockhead, Bo Zack and his little brother Zo Black.

As soon as White Timmy looked up and saw Shitty, Squirt and Lil E heading in their direction, he yelled, "What you alley boys shooting?" He called them the name they call their crew.

"Whatever!" Shitty yelled back as he got directly in the dice game.

"My shot!" Shitty said, grabbing the green dice as Blockhead missed his number. "Who got me!"

"I got you good shooter," White Timmy said.

"Nah, I got my backs!" Blockhead yelled at White Timmy. "Shoot your shot." Shitty rolled the dice, his first roll hit a seven, then an eight, his second shot making his point an eight.

10

RICO | KINGS OF THE YO

"Who don't like him?" Squirt yelled to whoever wanted to go against Shitty.

"I don't like him for a hunnid," said a tall Julio Jones, (the wide receiver from the Atlanta Falcons) look-a-like that Shitty, Squirt or Lil E had never seen before.

"It's a bet," Squirt said. "Anybody else tryna bet before he throws dis motherfucker on the bucks?" Squirt continued.

"I don't like his dirty ass for fifty fatback Kane," Zo Black said to Squirt calling him a nickname he made up for him.

"It's a bet, Zo. Shoot your shot, bruh," Squirt said to Shitty.

Shitty started shaking the dice and talking shit like he always do while looking at Squirt and Lil E, Shitty yelled, "What's dem niggas hood we fucked up so much dat dey don't come outside no more?"

"Fifty third!" They all said at the same time as Shitty rolled the dice talking about a hood in North east D.C. called Clay Terrace.

Shitty went straight out wit' a six-one, but as soon as Blockhead went to grab the money off the ground, in a blink of an eye Shitty whipped out a black and silver Mac 10. machine gun with a 50-round magazine from under his Helly Hanson ski coat and grabbed Blockhead by the collar of his shirt pointing the Mac 10. in his face. As soon as Lil E and Squirt saw Shitty make his move they both pulled out a Glock 30. with 30 round magazines and pointed them at everyone at the dice game.

"Y'all already know wat time it is!" Shitty yelled, looking at Blockhead in his eyes seeing nothing but fear.

"Damn, Fatback Kane you going rob me?" Zo Black said to Squirt with tears in his eyes.

"Nah, get the fuck Zo! Hurry up!" Squirt yelled, shaking his head side to side.

"Come on, Bo Zack!" Zo Black yelled to his brother.

11

Bo Zack started walking toward Zo Black.

"Fuck no," Squirt said, pointing his Glock at Bo Zack and Zo Black.

"Now, since your friendly ass wanna be Superman, you ain't going nowhere!" Squirt yelled to Zo Black.

"But dis my brother, Fatback Kane!" Zo Black yelled.

"Well, you 'bout to get robbed with him. Get the fuck on the wall," Squirt said, pointing his Glock at Zo face.

Squirt, Shitty, and Lil E started making the group of eight empty their pockets and get on their knees. As everybody started getting on their knees Lil E spotted the tall Julio Jones look-a-like tryna take a step to the side like he was about to try something.

"Your Julio Jones lookin' ass try to run. You gonna catch something other than footballs!" Lil E yelled as he grab the Julio Jones look-a-like, threw him to the ground and kicked him in the face.

Lil E then one by one, checked everyone's pocket's, waist, socks and even briefs until he felt he had everything they had on them. While Shitty and Squirt stood there back to back guns in hand. Squirt watched everything around them as Shitty made sure none of their victims ran or tried anything. After successfully robbing everybody Shitty made them all lay flat on their stomachs with their eyes closed until they made their exit.

As they walked off from the robbery laughing, Shitty asked, "Where Sway and Day-Day at? I ain't seen dem niggas all day."

"I saw lips, he said dey was around Edgewood, but dey was on dey way around here. But that was three hours ago. They should be in the trap by now," Squirt said.

"A'ight we might as well go to da trap and see is dey in dere. I got to put this Mac up and we got to split this money anyway," Shitty said.

12

"Bet," Squirt and Lil E said at the same time as they all headed back up the Yo to their trap.

●　●　●　●　●　●

In the trap Day-Day, Sway, Flip and Fats were just doing their normal waiting for fiends, talking shit, smoking, and watching gangster movies. Day-Day and Sway, nineteen-year-old, identical twin brothers were only two minutes apart. The only way to tell them apart if you ain't really know them was that Sway has a mole on the side of his ear. Day-Day and Sway share the same dark skin, the same 5'5 height and the same weight of one-hundred and thirty-five pounds. They both also rocked low haircuts, other than looks they didn't have too much more in common. Day-Day is a quick temper, shoot first, ask questions never type guy, while sway is more the laid back, get money type. However, both when needed will let their guns off without a second thought.

Flip is the oldest in their circle at twenty-one-years old. Flip is 6'1, brown-skinned, slim build weighing one-hundred and eighty pounds, with a low haircut. He is laid back and all about his money and bitches, but just like his crew of goons he lives for some gunplay.

"Damn, Day-Day you gonna keep lookin' at the same movies? Put something else on," Flip yelled to Day-Day entering the living room from the kitchen breaking up some dro in a $50 bill, taking a seat next to Day-Day and Sway on the couch.

Nigga you better get da fuck outta here! I brought this T.V. in here. You can go down bottom in YaYa house," Day-Day replied talking about another trap house down the street where Flip mainly be at.

"Yeah, whatever. Fuck that TV. I'll break that motherfucker. I bet you wanna hit this dro," Flip said to Day-Day as he was lighting up the dro.

"You ain't going to break shit, and fuck dat weak ass shit. I'm waiting for Moore to pull up anyway to get some purp," Day-Day replied.

"Y'all niggas loud as shit, sir," Fats said entering the living room from the back bedroom.

Fats was an older dude that they be around sometimes due to them hanging and hustling in the alley, but that was about it. Fats was at least twelve to fifteen years their senior and put you in the mindset of *Big Worm* from the movie *Friday*, but only in looks. Fats was one of the scariest niggas you will meet, but cool as shit and would get him some money.

"You talking about we loud as shit. You was in dere snoring loud as shit," Sway said to Fats.

They all broke out laughing.

Knock! Knock! Knock!

Someone banged on the front door getting their attention.

"Answer the door, Sway!" Day-Day yelled.

"You could have answered it, you're the closest one," Sway said, getting up to answer the door shaking his head.

"Damn, let me hit that loud. That shit smells good as shit!" Shitty yelled as he, Lil E, and Squirt entered the trap house giving everybody dap and smelling the dro Flip just lit up in the air.

"Damn, where da fuck y'all been all day?" Flip said to Shitty as he passed him the blunt of dro.

"Shiddd, we just came from robbing da dice game down Double R, kill. Dem niggas was scared as shit," Squirt said laughing. "Damn, y'all ain't call my phone. What type of wild shit y'all on?" Day-Day was mad that he ain't get in on the action.

Nigga your goofy ass brother said y'all was around Edgewood and that shit was spur of the moment. Turk called Lil E's phone and said dey was down dere gambling, so we went down dere and bagged the whole game," Shitty said as he puffed the dro three times and passed it to Squirt.

"So, y'all bagged Turk?" Sway and Flip both said at the same time as they both start smiling.

"Nah, we told him step off and robbed everyone else," Lil E said, smiling as Squirt passed him the blunt of dro.

"So, who da fuck was at the crap game?" Day-Day said still a little upset about not being around to da hit move.

"Shid Blockhead, White Timmy, Bo Zack, and four other niggas dat we ain't never seen before," Shitty said. "But guess who else was down dere? Y'all going to laugh like shit," Shitty continued laughing.

"Who?" Day-Day, Sway and Flip all said, looking at Shitty smiling, wondering who they robbed knowing Shitty it could be anybody.

"Zo Black," Shitty said, everybody in the trap busted out laughing but Fats.

"Damn, sir, y'all robbed Zo Black?" Fats said to Shitty shocked and upset by what he had just heard.

Zo Black was part of Fats inner circle and sold drugs for Fats. On top of that, he hangs on 37th Street in the middle which they call da alley with Shitty and the rest of his crew along with Lips, Mack, Turk, Bo and Baby Boy. Zo Black was one of the funniest niggas you'd meet and played for a vocal gogo band named M.O.B which stands for Money Over Bitches. Zo Black's nineteen-years-old, black as tar, 5'6, one-hundred and thirty pounds and one of the scariest niggas in the hood, but still a good dude.

"Nigga I know dats your man, Fats. I told him to roll out when we whipped out our dogs, but he tried to tell his brother Bo Zack to come with him. Tryna play superman, so we robbed him, his brother and da rest of dem niggas, fuck it," Squirt said to Fats not really caring about robbing Zo Black or how Fats felt about it.

"That's crazy tho, dats Zo Black, sir. How much money did he have on him? Because he still owes me a gee for an ounce I gave him." Fats looked at Shitty shaking his head, feeling he was the reason they robbed Zo Black.

"I don't know. We ain't count it yet, plus, we put all dem niggas money together. Matter of fact, come on y'all lets go count dat shit and split it," Shitty said to Squirt and Lil E heading to the back bedroom with them on his heels.

"Where the fuck, KGR and Loc?" Day-Day yelled to his crew as he, Sway and Flip followed them in the back bedrooms as Fats left out the trap mad.

"I don't know. Dey said dey was about go find a move earlier before we hit' our move," Shitty said as Lil E cleared his socks and pockets of all the money they took from the robbery.

"Everybody grab some money and count that shit it'll be quicker," Lil E said to his crew grabbing a handful of $100 bills.

"I sure hope KGR and Loc dumb ass came off and ain't get locked up or do nothing stupid." Shitty said as him and everyone in his crew shook their heads, knowing with KGR and Loc together without anyone else in their crew something stupid was bound to happen.

CHAPTER 2

"Ay, bra. Ay, bra!" KGR yelled twice trying to get lock attention.

Loc was trying to holla at a bad, red bone girl walking down the street with a baby.

"So, damn you ain't gonna stop? Fuck you den, bitch and your little son!" Loc said to the red-bone girl, then turning his attention to KGR. "What Moe? You all yellin' in my ear and shit. You see I was tryna get dat little bitch."

"Nigga, whatever," KGR said caring less about Loc trying to hook up with a girl when they was supposed to be trying to find a move.

KGR and Loc walked on 34th Street N.E. about two and a half blocks from their hood.

"Bra you tryna rob slim right dere in front of that building? He probably sellin' coke or weed," KGR said, pointing to a fat, light-skinned dude in all black in front of a building about thirty yards ahead of them.

"I don't give a fuck. Come on," Loc said, looking at KGR like the answer to his question was a no brainer.

As KGR and Loc got a few steps in front of the building they saw another dude with a red hoodie come out of the building, and stand next to the fat, light-skinned dude they had their eyes on. Loc and KGR headed in front of the building with one thing on their minds, money.

"Ay, Slim! It's some loud out here?" KGR said to the dude that they already had their eyes on.

"Yeah! What y'all little niggas want?" The fat, light-skinned dude said.

"Y'all got some dubs?" KGR said.

"We got whatever y'all want," said the dude with the red hoodie. "We even got schoolbooks for y'all lil' asses," he continued, laughing and pulling out a pound of dro.

"You got jokes?" KGR said, giving a fake laugh. "We cool on da school shit. But let us get all dat loud and shit," KGR continued, he pulled out his Glock .30 as Loc quickly followed suit, pointing them at both of their vicks.

"Holddd up, shorty what da fuck going on!" The fat, light-skinned dude yelled. "I ain't even from round here."

"Shut da fuck. We don't give a fuck where you from!" KGR yelled and slapped him in the face with his Glock, then grabbed him and started checking his pockets, taking every and anything in them.

"I just came outside, I ain't got nothing to do with nothing," the dude with the red hoodie said, fear in his eyes.

"Oh, dis shit ain't funny no more, huh?" Loc said, laughing and taking the pound of dro out his hands, then everything out his pockets including some Honda car keys attached to an alarm system.

"Come on, bra, we gone," KGR said to Loc as he slapped the fat, light-skinned dude again in his head causing him to fall to the ground.

Pop! Pop! Pop!

Loc shot the dude with the red hoodie in the chest three times.

"Thanks for da back to school money," Loc said laughing and walking off fast, while KGR started jogging.

"Come da fuck on. Fuck you doing?" KGR yelled at Loc noticing him walking fast pointing at something small in his hand.

"I got his car keys. I'm tryna see where da fuck the car at?" Loc said, pointing the alarm at any Honda car he saw.

"Come on, bra! Dat car could be anywhere. I'm gone," KGR said about to run off until he heard the alarm sound off.

Bleep! Bleep!

"I found it," Loc said, joggin' towards the dark tinted black-on-black Honda pilot truck, getting in.

"Open da motherfuckin' door! Hurry up," KGR said running to the passenger side of the truck.

"Nah, run off like you was about to do," Loc said starting up the truck.

"Moe, it ain't no time to be playing kill, hit the lock."

"Haa Haa your 'noid ass," Loc said, laughing and hitting the lock, letting KGR get in the truck.

"A'ight pull the fuck off. You can do dat shit later!" KGR yelled as Loc was trying to find a CD to put in the stereo.

"Shut da fuck up. I should've left your ass," Loc said, laughing and pulling off in the truck heading back to their hood.

* * * * * *

As Loc and KGR pulled back around the Yo and rode past where they hang, they could see that da alley was live and almost everybody was out tonight down the bottom of 37th Street by a school called Sousa. As soon as they both got out of the truck they headed straight to where they hang. As they are walking past building 300 which sits in the middle of the alley and down bottom KGR busts out nowhere.

"Why da fuck you start hitting for?"

"Cause he was purpin, fuck dat bitch ass nigga," Loc said.

"Dats a body for nothing if we get bagged," KGR said, shaking his head as they made it to where their crew was. "What's up with y'all?" KGR said to no one in particular dapping everybody up.

"What da fuck you looking all mad for?" Squirt asked his little brother noticing something was on his mind.

Squirt was standing with Flip, Baby Boy, Mac, Mello, Sway and Day-Day. Baby Boy was Sway and Day-Day's brother. He was one year older than them at nineteen-years-old. He was 5'7, dark-skinned, one-hundred and forty-five pounds, with a low Caesar like haircut and weave in it. Baby Boy was laid back for the most part, but will let his gun go off. Mello is the cousin of Shitty, Lil E and Loc. He was twenty-one-years old, six-feet tall, one-hundred and eighty pounds. He was brown- skinned with a low haircut with a weave in it. Mello wasn't from the alley, he is from down bottom of 37th and rep it hard. Mello was trigger happy as hell and could care less about anybody's feelings, other than the niggas he hang with. Mack is Shitty, Lil E and Loc's uncle, the little brother of their mother and the cousin of Squirt and KGR on his father's side of the family. He is 5'9', two-hundred and twenty pounds and chubby, brown-skinned with a low haircut and a fade in the back of his big ass head. Mack would fight anybody, but when it came to gun play, he ain't want no parts of nothing.

"This wild ass nigga Loc just hit a nigga down thirty-fourth for nothing," KGR said, still upset that Loc started shooting.

"Nigga you still trippin? Dat shit over now and slim was talkin' reckless. Fuck that nigga," Loc said, not caring what anybody felt about his actions.

"Who the fuck y'all hit?" Day-Day asked.

"Some niggas down thirty-fourth that we bagged. We asked him if he had some loud for sell and dat nigga talking 'bout he got some school supplies for our little asses. Then he started laughin' and shit. So, I gave his bitch ass something to laugh about," Loc said and everybody busted out laughing, except KGR he ain't see nothing funny.

"What y'all come off with?" Squirt said.

"A pound of loud, like four bands and a black Honda truck with tints and dubs on it," Loc said smiling.

"Dat was y'all in the black on black pilot dat just rode pass?" Flip asked talking 'bout the Honda truck that passed them minutes ago.

"Yeah, dat was us," KGR said.

"Where y'all park dat joint?" Mello asked

"Down bottom!" Loc yelled.

"Den y'all just hit a nigga in dat joint? Y'all need to go move dat joint off a frontline and don't be riding dat joint around, real live," Mello said.

"Go move dat joint KGR," Loc said, trying to hand him the truck keys.

"Nigga, I'm not 'bout to go move shit. You the one took dat hot ass joint!" KGR yelled at Loc.

"I'll go move it. Shiddd, we gonna use dat joint to go out and go thur in," Flip said, taking the keys from Loc and jogging off down bottom to move the truck.

"Where the fuck is Lil E and Shitty?" Baby Boy asked Loc.

"I don't know," Loc said, shrugging his shoulder.

"Shitty just went down Stoneridge to his girl's house. He said he was in for da day," Squirt said.

"And I don't know where Lil E at," Squirt continued.

"What da fuck time is it?" Sway asked.

"It's only seven-thirty p.m., Sir," Mack said, looking at his iPhone10. "Shitty went in early as shit. His dirty ass must be up," he continued.

21

"Yeah, he a'ight. We bagged Double R earlier for some slight shit." Squirt laughed.

"I heard y'all came off," Baby Boy said.

"We hit for like ten and some change," Squirt answered smiling.

"Ay police just jumped in the circle!" Flip yelled behind them coming down the steps that leads to the top of 37th Place and Circle.

"I'm goin' in, Mack drop me off," Squirt stated.

"What you doing, KGR?"

"Shid, I'm goin' in," KGR said as him, Squirt and Mack gave everybody dap and started walking off to Mack's car.

"Drop me off down bottom, Mack," Mello said walking off with them.

"I'm gonna see y'all later, too. I'm 'bout to go up Mudda joint," Baby Boy said, referring to his girl's house.

"A'ight," Flip said, giving Baby Boy dap. "What y'all 'bout to do?" Loc asked the rest of his crew.

"I'm 'bout to go back in da trap. I don't know what da twins gonna do. I'm tryna finish this coke I got left," Flip told Loc.

"Shid, we 'bout to do the same shit," Day-Day said speaking for him and Sway.

"Well, I'm 'bout to go in my grand mova house. I'ma see y'all tomorrow," Lock said, giving everybody dap as he stepped off heading to his grandmother house as they headed to the trap for the night.

● ● ● ● ● ●

"Ay, Mook. What's up?" Shitty asked his girl as he stepped through the door of her house.

"Shit, boo, just g'tting' out of the shower waiting on you to come in."

Mook has been Shitty's girlfriend since he was fifteen-years-old. They had been through as much as anybody in a relationship of three and a half years. Mook even did a two-year bid with Shitty when he was a juvenile for a robbery he and Squirt committed, but he was the only one who got locked up for it. Mook and Shitty has had their share of ups and downs, but anyone that knows Shitty knows she's his heart and vice versa. Mook is a year younger than Shitty at eighteen-years-old. She is 5'6, one-hundred and forty pounds and a redbone with the sexiest lips. Mook reminds you of Rocsi Diaz with a Nia long haircut and a Rihanna like body.

"You musta been waiting for the dick all day," Shitty teased gripping her ass.

"You already know. I've been waiting and talking about this dick since this morning after you punished this pussy and sent me to work," she admitted grabbing his dick through his pant.

"Damn, you teasin' like shit. What you waiting for?" Shitty laughed while at the same time unbuckling and unzipping his pants.

"You nasty." Mook smiled, dropped to her knees and pulled his boxer briefs down exposing his dick, then put it in her mouth.

She sucked and licked his dick like it would be her last time. Mook was sucking so viciously that he had to literally pry her head away so he could not cum, just yet.

"Hold on, boo, let's go in the bedroom," Shitty requested as he pushed her head away from his dick.

"A'ight, come on. You know I hate stopping when I'm suckin' your dick," Mook reminded with an attitude. She grabbed Shittys' hand and tried to escort him to their bedroom.

"Look go head and get comfortable, I'm 'bout to come in dere right behind you," he said letting go of her hand.

"A'ight, hurry up, boo."

As soon as Mook went in the room Shitty grabbed his pants and dug in his pocket to get an E pill he had brought earlier from Mello. He popped the pill and headed straight to his bedroom to fuck his girl's lights out. Stepping into his bedroom, he saw Mook's flawless body laying across their queen-sized bed with her legs spread wide open. She was playing with her shaved, pretty, pussy. He walked over dick still out and began waving it in front of her face in a teasing way.

"Stop playin', boy."

"Sike nah, here." Shitty laughed as he let her take his dick into her mouth.

She started sucking, then licking his balls just how he'd taught her to from the bottom to the top she licked and sucked. Taking his dick out of her mouth, he sat on the end of the bed, grabbed her perfectly manicured feet and put one in his mouth slowly flickering his tongue all over her toes, licking the sole from top to bottom. He put all her toes in his mouth at one time while massaging the other foot. Letting go of her foot, Shitty watched as she gradually spread her thick thighs, which only made him hornier, causing him to slowly lick his way up to her shaved, pink pussy flicking his tongue around the outer lips. She started pushing his head down, wanting him to really get to work. Resisting, he continued teasing her with a couple more licks, parting her juicy lips and licking around inside her sweet tasting pussy while rubbing her clit, making her reach an orgasm immediately.

"Mmm, boo, I'm comin'! Oh, my god! Maudarico, it's so good!" Mook screamed, calling Shitty by his birth name.

Knowing he had her up against the ropes, he stuck his finger in her ass ramming it in and out. Feeling the penetration, she grinded harder against his face releasing all her juices in his mouth. After she came, Shitty commanded her to get up and get in the doggy style position so he could fuck her from the back. He plunged into her wet pink pussy from the back fucking her with long, slow, and deep strokes as she threw her ass back.

"Damn, it's so good! I'm 'bout to cum, Mook," Shitty moaned like a girl. The fuck faces and the tightness of her pussy made him cum fast. Mook sensed he was about to cum and she threw her ass back harder, demanding he fuck her harder. Digging in and out, faster and harder Shitty felt himself cumming. As he took his dick out and shot his cum all over her ass, she quickly turned around and sucked him dry. Feeling relieved he laid back on the bed while she went to get a washcloth to clean him up. After cleaning him she jumped in the bed, wrapped her arm around him and gave him a kiss.

"Why you looking at me like that?" Mook asked, confused because Shitty was looking at her shaking his head side to side.

"Cause you got a torch," Shitty said.

Mook playfully punched him, they both laughed and laid back with their eyes closed and fell asleep.

CHAPTER 3

The next day down bottom Mello, Shy, Guala, Eroc and Leeky was just chillin' standing in front of building 324 as usual selling drugs and talking shit it was only 2:30 p.m. in the afternoon and the temperature was at least 37 degrees, but felt below 0.

"Damn, Moe, it's cold as shit out here," Shy complained.

Shy is seventeen-years-old, 5'6, one-hundred and thirty pounds, brown-skinned with a low haircut and a Muslim-like beard. Shy was originally from the alley, but started hanging down bottom with Mello due to him living where everybody hangs and not wanting his grandmother all in his business. Shy was still an alley boy. Shy is laid back for the most part, but will rob and shoot here and there.

Guala is twenty-years-old, 5'8, one-hundred and sixty pounds, light-brown skinned with a low haircut and Muslim-like beard also. Guala is a sneaky, get with type dude. He just wanted to be down with any and everything to prove he wasn't a scary dude when in reality he is. But he's cool and will bust his gun. Leeky is twenty-years-old, 5'10, one hundred seventy pounds, brown-skinned with a low haircut and a goatee. Leeky is a good dude for the most part, he's laid back and just trying to get some money and fuck with bitches. Eroc is twenty-one-years old, 5'9, one-hundred and sixty-five pounds, dark-brown skinned, with shoulder length dreadlocks. Eroc is the baby brother of Baby Boy, Lips, Sway and Day-Day. He will bust his gun, but is laid back.

"Kill, dey say it's supposed to be like dis all day," Leeky said, taking his gloves out his pockets and putting them on.

"Y'all keep cryin' and shit. Go in da mutherfuckin house if y'all cold!" Eroc yelled before he stepped off to go catch a crack sell.

"Dat nigga lunchin'. It's cold as shit out here. But I'm not going nowhere. I'm tryna go buy dis Versace fit I saw for the La Pearl tomorrow night," Shy informed Mello.

"Yeah, I hear you. I'm out here all day. You know I like dis shit," Mello replied laughin'.

"Y'all hear 'bout Shitty, Squirt, Flip and Day-Day fuckin up Simple City last night?" Guala asked as Eroc walked back up.

"Yeah, I saw Squirt fat ass dis morning. Him and Lil E was comin' out of Kenny's house. He said dey dropped like thirty and hit like four people around dere," Mello recalled smiling.

"Dem niggas be wildin, kill. I saw KGR and Loc dis morning when I came out. Dey was driving Shitty's blue Chrysler three-hundred. Dey said dey was about to go see who was outside around paradise so dey could fuck dat joint up with the Mac. I told dem niggas dey could go head, it's too early for me," Shy said as if it being too early was the only reason he ain't go with Loc and KGR.

"Dey doing dem," Mello said.

"Y'all got y'all dogs on y'all?"

"Yeah, I got mines," Leeky said, referring to the black and silver Glock .26 He had in his 550 North face coat pocket.

"You already know I got my joint." Guala pulled out his P.90 Ruger 45.

"Y'all ain't got no joint on y'all?" Mello asked Eroc and Shy noticing they ain't respond to his question the first time.

"Nah, I'm 'bout to go get Lips joint, I'll be back," E-roc said jogging off to get his brother's gun.

"Lil Kevin got my joint, I'm 'bout to tell him to bring it right here," Shy said pulling out his phone to call little Kevin.

"You ain't seen Shitty today?" Mello asked Guala.

"Nah, I'm 'bout to call his phone," Guala answered.

"A'ight, I'm 'bout to go up YaYa joint real quick and bag dis loud up," Mello said going inside of building 324 upstairs to their trap.

"A'ight bra," Guala said as he pulled out his phone and dial Shitty's number.

On the second ring Shitty answered, "Yo-Yo," Shitty said.

"What's up, brah?" Guala asked.

"What it do?"

"Shit cooling, where you at?"

"I'm 'bout to pull up back around there. I just came from White Corner with Day-Day."

"Yeah, I heard y'all dropped Steph last night," Guala said excited, but was cut off by Leeky.

"Ay, brah, I'm 'bout to go to the ice cream truck real quick," Leaky said to Guala in the background.

"A'ight!" Guala yelled.

"Yeah, brah," Guala said back in his phone.

"Who the fuck was that?" Shitty asked

"That was leaky," Guala replied.

"Oh, yeah. He got dat glizzy on him?" Shitty said, referring to Leaky's Glock 26.

"Yep, kill he do," Guala said, laughing already knowing what Shitty was up to.

"Look, I'm bout to come down there. Make sure he don't step off, real live."

"A'ight, I got you." Guala hung up as Leeky walked back up smoking a Newport 100.

"Let me hit that," Guala said to Leeky as he passed him the cigarette.

"What the fuck Shitty talkin' 'bout?" Leeky asked.

"Shit, he talkin' 'bout some little bitches dats supposed to be comin' thru da alley or whatever," Guala lied just making small talk so he could keep him still for a minute until Shitty arrived.

"Yeah, that's what's up. Look, I'm 'bout to go in YaYa's house for a minute and get warm. It's cold as shit out here," Leeky said.

"Hold right quick, I'm 'bout to go up there, too. Let me make two more sells," Guala said, trying to get him to stay put.

"A'ight."

Dat nigga Shitty needs to hurry up before I let dis nigga roll out, Guala thought.

"What's up with y'all?" Shitty said to shy, Guala and Leeky making Guala and Leeky reach for their guns catchin' them off guard.

Shitty was still with Day-Day, they came through the back door of building 324 to get right up on them and to catch them by surprise.

"What's sup wit y'all?" Shy gave Shitty and Day-day dap.

Finally breaking his long silence. "Y'all niggas need to stop creepin' like that. Y'all know we beefin' hard. Y'all gonna fuck around and make a nigga accidentally shoot one of y'all," Guala said, shaking his head mad that they scared him.

"Nigga you shoot one of us by accident, you're gonna accidentally die out here," Day-Day said as he and Shitty started laughing.

"Leeky, let me see dat joint," Shitty requested trying get the Glock out of his hands.

"Dis my brovas' Block," Leeky said, pulling out the 2 tone Glock 26, handing it to Shitty.

"Dis little joint pretty is shit." Shitty turned the Glock side to side in his hand admiring its beauty. Checking the cup and backin' out of arm's reach Shitty said, "Leeky tell Block I'm in da alley if he feel some type of way. Good lookin', brah."

"Damn, Sir! Me though?" Leeky said, shocked Shitty would take his gun since they'd grown up together.

"I ain't tryin hear that shit," Shitty dismissed him. "Day-Day, we gone."

"Hold up, bra! Guala what type of dog is that?" Day-Day said referring to his gun.

"Y'all got me fuck up!" Guala yelled.

"Nah, you got us fucked up!" Da-da yelled whipping out his all black Glock .27, as Shitty pointed the Glock 26 he still had in his hand at Guala's face.

"Oh, yeah, Shitty?" Guala said thrown off by Shitty pointing a Glock at his face after he had held Leeky outside in the cold so he could take his gun.

Not caring about how Guala felt Shitty just smiled and said, "You already know what's up."

"Now put ur motherfuckin' hands up, and don't move 'fore I smoke your bitch ass," Day-Day threatened and Guala obliged without hesitation knowing Day-Day would shoot him without a second thought. "Shy take that dog up off him!" Day-Day yelled. Shy did as he was told. "A'ight come on Shy we gone now. Now accidentally shoot a nigga," Day-Day said him, Shy and Shitty laughed as they jogged off heading to da alley.

* * * * * *

Squirt and Flip pulled up down bottom and parked in Squirt's silver 97 Camaro SS. With the T. Tops they got out and walked toward building 324 where everybody be at. They saw Mello, Guala, Leeky and Eroc standing in front of the building talking loud as shit and by the looks on their faces they could tell something had just happened, but they never would've guessed it was what they was about to hear.

"Fuck is up with y'all? Why y'all look like somebody just got raped?" Squirt said to all of them laughing.

"Nigga, ain't shit funny dem niggas just took our guns," Guala fumed getting in Squirt's face.

"Y'all go head on with that shit," Flip said getting between them.

"Naw, this nigga actin' like he wants some smoke. Talking to me like I'ma little ass boy or something. Like he don't know what the fuck is up with me!" Squirt yelled, looking Guala straight in his face ready to work.

"Bra, leave dat shit alone for me," Mello requested because he already knew once Squirt got mad he wasn't trying to hear nothing.

"Yeah, on the strength of you, bra. I'ma leave dat shit alone," Squirt agreed still looking at Guala who was now looking scared to death because deep down he knew he couldn't do nothing with Squirt on no level.

"Nah, that's my bad Squirt. Dat shit ain't for us. A nigga just mad as shit right now cause Shitty and Day-Day just snaked me and Leeky for our dogs," Guala said still mad but copping at the same time.

"Damn, dem niggas did that wild shit for real?" Flip acted surprised.

"Yeah, they just did it like an hour ago while I was up YaYa's house. Dey knew I would've never let dem do no shit like dat if I was out here," Mello said to Flip and Squirt.

See situations like that put Squirt in fucked up predicaments because Squirt, Flip and Mello was like brothers. They always be together fucking with bitches and chilling. The only thing was that Mello was from down bottom and he repped that shit to the fullest, but that wasn't the issue. The problem was that he was the only one down bottom that had heart and would shoot his gun no matter what. The rest of the D. Boys was scared as shit. But being as though they were his men, he felt like he had to protect them all the time.

"C'mon, bra, let's go holla at dem and see if I can get them dogs back," Mello instructed Squirt knowing he could possibly get them back.

"A'ight," Squirt agreed, shaking his head as they walked to the car.

One thing he knew about his crew was once they robbed you it wasn't no giving nothing back period no matter who you was.

* * * * * *

"Ay, you should've seen dat nigga Guala's face when we whipped out on his goofy ass. He gonna say we got him fucked up," Day-Day explained to Lil E laughin' like shit.

Day-Day, Lil E, Sway, Shitty and Shy were all sitting in the alley chilling and hustling as if they didn't just rob Leeky and Guala an hour ago.

"Ay, Shitty let me have dis glizzy since I'm the only one dat ain't got one," Shy said, hoping he would let him get the Glock they'd just got off Leeky.

"You can hold it down, I ain't trippin," Shitty said, handing Shy the glizzy, but never saying he can actually have it.

"Good lookin', bra. So, who y'all want me to give dis big ass P.90 to?" Shy asked Shitty and Day-Day talking about the Ruger 45 that he'd just taken off Guala.

RICO | KINGS OF THE YO

"Shid you might as well put that big motherfucker in the brick wall," Day-Day said talking 'bout the stash stop they had in the alley, where they often hid guns and drugs when it was hot outside.

"Ay, where dat nigga Squirt at?" Shitty asked Lil E.

"I don't know, I talked to him earlier and him and Flip was together. But I don't know where dey was at," Lil E said.

"Dats crazy y'all just spoke dem nigga up. Cause dats dem pullin' up in Squirt's car right dere," Shitty said, pointing to the front of the alley.

"Awww, man, dey got Mello with dem. So, y'all already know what he 'bout to say," Sway said as Mello, Squirt, and Flip got out the car and walked to the alley where they were sitting.

"What's sup wit' y'all?" Squirt said dapping everybody up.

"Shit coolin'. Fuck y'all comin' from?" Shitty asked.

"We just came from down bottom where y'all just did dat wild shit!" Mello yelled at Shitty mad they took guns from the niggas he be with every day.

"Nigga you comin' up here purpin? Leeky don't need dat joint. He ain't gonna kill nothin' or let nothin' die!" Shitty yelled back at Mello. "And we wasn't even gonna take Guala joint until his scared ass started bluffin'," Shitty continued.

"It don't matter. Y'all comin' down bottom with dat bullshit startin' shit. Y'all gonna make a nigga fuck dis joint up," Mello said.

"Nigga, you fakin' like shit. You got us fucked up. Y'all niggas ain't gonna fuck nothin' up," Day-Day said.

"Lil' twin stop playin' wit' me. You talkin' 'bout a nigga fakin'. I'll smack the shit out your lil' ass," Mello warned heated stepping closer to Day-Day.

"You got me fucked up!" Day-Day hollered as he whipped out his all black Glock .27 everybody in his crew followed suit whipping out there guns.

Taking a few steps back away from Day-Day, Mello said, "So, y'all gonna pull out dogs on me? And Shy your lil' scared ass was just down bottom with me all morning. So, you rockin' with these wild niggas?"

"You already know where I stand. I'm from da alley, I don't fuck wit' none of them niggas down there, but Eroc and…"

Shy was cut off by Shitty, "Bra, you ain't got to explain nothin' to dis nigga. He wanna keep saving dem scared ass niggas. Dem nigga some bitches real live," Shitty said to Shy mad he was trying to explain. "Matter of fact, since you said y'all fuck dis joint up, roll da fuck out!" Shitty yelled pointing his Mac-10 at Mello's chest.

"Yeah, cuz?" Mello raised his hands with anger in his eyes.

"Squirt you gonna let cuz point da Mac at me and tell me to roll out? Mello said.

"Dat's on y'all. You talkin' 'bout y'all will fuck something up," Squirt said, lookin' at Mello shaking his head.

"Say no more, fuck all y'all niggas. Y'all gonna see what's up!" Mello yelled as he ran off down bottom.

As Mello ran off Shitty and the rest of his crew put their guns back up.

"Kill Moe, I don't know who da fuck Mello thinks he is? Comin' up here like he Wayne Perry or somethin'," Shitty yelled at his crew. "Man, fuck dat, Wayne Perry ain't even dat bold to come up here like dat, kill," Day-Day said as everybody started laughin'.

"Kill bra, it's like one-fifty out here right now. Wayne Perry better bring Chin, Pimp and Kevin Gray wit' him and dey better all have on vests," Lil E said as everybody continued laughing.

"Y'all funny as shit, kill. Y'all know we beefin' wit down bottom now," Flip said, shaking his head side to side.

"Well, fuck it. Who we ain't beefin' wit?" Squirt said as if beefin' with down bottom now was nothing serious.

"Same shit, different day. I know one thing dem niggas better not get caught lackin'," Shitty said.

"Kill!" Everybody yelled almost at the same time as they all started walking to the trap.

CHAPTER 4

The next morning Shitty was driving his Blue 300c on Minnesota Avenue heading around a hood called Kenilworth in Northeast, D.C. with KGR and his little brother Loc. While driving on Minnesota Avenue and passing the subway station KGR out of blue turned down the radio.

"Ay, bra I head dem simp and Benning Park niggas be taking them niggas for bad around the worth," KGR said to Shitty.

"Oh, yeah?" Loc said surprised.

"Kill, dey say dem niggas be pullin' up 'round there robbing dem niggas and taking they dogs off dem on the regular," KGR said shaking his head.

"Shiddd, dats on dem. But dey wasn't goin' 'round dere before the twins and T. Loc got locked up. Now dat dey just came home all dat shit dead," Shitty explained to KGR talking about twin brothers Josh and Chris who came home from D.C. jail after beating a couple of shootings and murders.

"When the fuck Glock and dem come home bra?" Loc asked, shocked calling the twins by Glock a name they was known by, not knowing the twins beat they case and was now back on the streets.

"Dey just came home yesterday, but T. Loc still in. He had a mistrial but he's gonna beat dat shit kill. Dat's the only reason I'm riding 'round dere now, to holla at B. Love and Day-Day if dey out dere. Pocko and 2-Tie locked up and I don't fuck wit' the rest of dem niggas like dat," Shitty said, turning the radio back up listening to that new little *Money Bagg Yo Time Served* CD, while making a left turn on Nallen Helen Borough.

After a few minutes Shitty, KGR and Loc were pulling up, up top around Kenilworth. As Shitty pulled up he saw one of the twins, not exactly knowing which one from the distance talking to a girl named Robin that talk to his man Day-Day. Shitty parked and he, KGR and Loc got out the car and walking toward Robin and the twin. He noticed it was Josh. Josh was twenty-years-old, 5'10, one-hundred and ninety pounds, brown-skinned with dreads that hang pass his chest, his twin Chris was exactly the same. Chris and Josh were four minutes apart and identical twins. Chris was more laid back, his brother Josh was the total opposite. Both of them was a shoot first, ask questions never, type of dude. Neither one had no picks on who they robbed or get into it with. If they ain't fuck with you it was whatever, whenever with whoever. Robin is just a little light-skinned, eighteen-year-old hood rat that was from around Kenilworth who fucked with Day-Day now. Just two-years ago she fucked with Day-Day's brother Baby Boy. She was 5'5, one-hundred and twenty-five pounds, with a tight body.

"Glock, what's up, bra? Welcome home, Slim. I see y'all finally beat dat shit," Shitty said as he, KGR and Loc walked up and gave Josh dap.

"Yeah, bra. Kill A nigga just did a brick over dat jail. I see you lookin' sweet though. What's up, y'all?" Josh said dapping Shitty, KGR and Loc, smiling.

37

"Shit, I just came 'round here to see can I get up on you. Matter fact, hun," Shitty said, giving Josh a handful of money.

"Good lookin', bra. How much is dis?" Josh said puttin' the money in his pocket.

"Like fifteen hundred, some short shit to keep your fronts up for right now," Shitty said smiling.

"Appreciate you, slim," Josh said dappin Shitty a second time.

"Damn, what's up Shitty, KGR and Loc? What y'all niggas can't speak," Robin said with her hand on her hip with a fake mean mug on her face.

"Oh, what's up, Robin?" Shitty said as he, KGR and Loc gave her a hug.

"Where my, boo, Day-Day at y'all," Robin said smiling.

"We don't know, he ain't right here. You got his number call him," Loc said getting smart.

"Fuck you, lil' Malik. You always getting smart," Robin said, rolling her eyes calling Loc by his birth name.

"Y'all funny as shit. Glock where B. Love wild ass at?" Shitty asked Josh, laughing.

"He over dere gambling." Josh pointed toward a front porch with a group of about six people shooting dice. "Come on, y'all," Josh said and they started walking to the dice game.

Robin walked the opposite way. As they got close to the dice game B. Love noticed Shitty, KGR and Loc walking up with Josh.

"Ay, Shittyyyy!" B. Love yelled being extra.

"What's up, Moe?" B. Love was twenty-one-years old, 5'10, one-hundred and ninety-five pounds, brown-skinned with dreads that hang to his navel. B. Love was a cool dude that just like to get money.

"Damn, Love, you extra as shit Moe, Kill," Shitty said, smiling.

"You callin' this man name like that loud as shit," Josh said to B. Love with a slight attitude.

"Dat shit ain't nothin'. What's up, Love?" Shitty said laughing.

"Where your fat ass man at?" B. Love asked Shitty talking about Squirt.

"Coolin' around the way, tryna run that bag up."

"Yeah, no question. I'ma holla at you in a minute before y'all leave. I'ma 'bout to go throw some numbers on these niggas real quick," B. Love said dapping Shitty up again, then walking off back to the dice game, leaving Josh, Shitty, KGR and Loc talking.

"Yeah, though Glock, I heard dem simp Benning Park niggas be taking dis joint for bad," Shitty said fucking with Josh knowing it would get under his skin.

"Nigga, you already know, you got me and bra fucked up, Kill! Dat shit dead, dem niggas was playing wit' dese scared ass niggas out here. You know me, bra and T. Loc was in. Dem niggas won't never play with dis joint now me and bra back, dey going get one of them crushed," Josh said to Shitty heated.

"I wish one of dem niggas would come around here," Josh continued venting.

"Yeah, I already know, but watch this," Shitty said.

"Ay, B. Love and y'all, ain't dat little Rocky and dem walkin' over here?" Shitty yelled to B. Love and the young boys he was gambling with.

"Where? Where at?" B. Love and another dude looked up from the dice game with fear in their eyes, looking all around, and putting their money in their pockets.

"Look, Glock, I told you dem niggas got dis joint shook. I'm gone back around the Yo," Shitty said as he, KGR, Loc and Josh started laughing hard is shit.

"Shitty you always playin' and shit," B. Love said.

"Shut your scary ass up. Dem niggas got y'all spooked out here!" Josh yelled to B. Love.

"I ain't scared of dem niggas. Dey ain't never rob me," B.Love said with his chest poked out.

"Yeah, whatever nigga. You was just scared ass shit," Josh taunted.

"Look, we gone," Shitty said, seeing that B. Love and Josh was about to get into it.

"Tell Chris hit my phone or y'all slide through da alley and fuck with me, B. Love got my number," Shitty said as him KGR and Loc dapped josh up.

"Ay, I'ma see your super scared ass later B. Love!" Shitty yelled, as he, KGR, and Loc walked to the car laughing.

Once inside the car Shitty looked at KGR and Loc as he started the car and up and cruised out of his parking spot.

Pulling up on the side of Josh and B. Love still arguing Shitty rolled his window down and said, "Ay, Glock and B. Love!"

"Yeah, bra?" They both yelled.

"Y'all already know I if y'all get too shook 'round here. Y'all can come hide around my joint. Y'all know I fucks with y'all, real live," Shitty said dead serious.

"You got me fucked up!" Josh yelled.

"Fuck it den," Shitty said and pulled off heading back around 37th with KGR and loc laughing.

* * * * * *

Later that Friday night the alley was live as shit. Shitty, Squirt, Flip, Baby Boy, Mac, Turk, Bo and Day-Day was chilling outside in the alley drinking, smoking and fucking with some little Clinton, Maryland bitches that Shitty called. Everybody was funning when Fats pulled up in his black suburban and got out.

"Ay, Mac and Bo let me holla at y'all right quick, Sir," Fats requested without acknowledging nobody else outside.

"What's up, Sir?" Bo asked when they walked across the street to the other alley.

Bo was Mac and Fats right hand man. He was 5'9, one-hundred and sixty-five pounds, brown-skinned with a haircut and looked like Chris Tucker. Bo acted hard, but was really scared to death, he was cool and loved to party.

"Man, y'all throwin' me off over dere fuckin' wit' dem youngins. Y'all know dey just robbed Zo?" Fats said.

"Man, dat ain't got nothin' to do wit' us. You know dem youngins gonna do dem regardless. I heard dat Squirt try to let him roll out and Zo put his cape on and tried be Superman for his brother," Mac said to Fats.

Fats turned and looked at Bo like, *is this nigga serious.*

"First off, Sir, dat shit ain't on just Zo because dat nigga had money on him dat he owed me. Den to make shit even more disrespectful even after I told dem dumb ass youngins dat he owed me, dey just looked at me like I was fuckin stupid," Fats said real mad at Mac.

"Yeah, dat is fucked up, sir. At least dey could've did was give you wat Zo owed you," Bo said siding with Fats like he always do. I feel you on dat. But dat shit still ain't got nothin' to do wit' me, slim or y'all. Zo got robbed so he still gotta pay you period!" Mac yelled, getting fed up with the conversation and wanting to get back to the bitches.

"Man, I'm just gettin tired of dem youngins, sir. I should go over dere and embarass one of their lil' asses and smack da shit out of dem," Fats said tryna hype himself up.

"Man, you must got a motherfuckin' bazooka in dat big ass truck because if you go over dere and smack one of dem youngins they gonna whip out dem glizzys and gun you down like a dog. And all dem got thirties on dem. Shitty got 50 in dat Mac," Mac said, getting scared because he knew that if

Fats did what he was talking about doing shit was going to get ugly fast!

"Man, fuck dem! You think dem youngins something and tryna save dem all the time because some of dem your people. But they can get backdoored just like anybody else," Fats said mad as shit now.

"Well, I tell you what. Y'all do y'all, I'm bout to go uptown wit' my BM cause I ain't got nothin' to do wit' dis shit, sir," Mac said, walking off to get in his car and go home because he knew shit was about to get crazy.

"Man, I'ma crush one of dem youngins. I'm tellin' you, slim," Fats said to Bo really in his feelings.

"Dat shit gonna be hard, sir. Dem youngins stay together at least two deep and you know for a fact dey got at least thirty on em," Bo said trying to get Fats to leave it alone without him sounding to scared.

"Just watch, sir, I got something for dey asses trust me," Fats said, smiling looking across the street at the youngins funnying in the alley.

CHAPTER 5

Leeky, Mello, Guala and Eroc were chilling downtown waiting for Fats to pull up so they could get some coke.

"Dere he go right dere, sir," Leeky said to Mello as Fats pulled up down bottom and parked.

Mello walked to the truck and got in. "What's up, sir?"

"Dat's an eight right dere," Fats said, handing Mello the coke and grabbing the money from Mello, putting it in his pocket.

"Good lookin', slim. But I need a favor," Mello said, tucking the coke in his coat.

"What's up, you want me to front you another eight?" Fats asked ready to look out for him.

"Naw, I'm cool on that, but I do need to hold a dog cause them niggas in the alley robbed Guala and Leeky for both of their dogs. Then they whipped out on me when I went up there and tried to get them back," Mello said getting mad just thinking about it.

Little did he know this was music to Fats' ears because now he had pawns he could use until he put his play together against the youngins.

"Oh, yeah, sir. Dem some wild niggas. Where was Flip and Squirt when dat shit happened? I know dem supposed to be your men right?" Fats said, seeing where Mello stood with them.

"Man, fuck Squirt! Dat nigga picked sides, and Flip ain't say nothin'. But I saw him after dat and he said he ain't got nothin' to do with it. I believe him, so we cool," Mello expressed hoping he could really trust Flip.

"Yeah, Flip gonna stay neutral. It's Squirt you gotta watch out for, he fucks wit' dem dudes tough. But look I'ma hit your phone in two hours and meet you down da blue house wit' a couple of dogs so y'all won't be bullshitting out here, slim." Fats dapped Mello up and pulled off after he got out the truck.

Fats was smiling because he finally saw a way to get the youngins out of the way without having to beef with them himself.

* * * * * *

The day finally came when down bottom and Da Alley Boys started officially beefing and surprisingly, the Alley Boys didn't start it.

"Man, ain't dat Shy bitch ass at the ice cream truck?" Guala asked Mello as they stood on the top of the steps of building 324 down bottom.

"Fuck yeah! Dat's his bitch ass. You got dat dog that I gave you?" Mello said, referring to the P.95 Ruger he got from Fats and gave Guala.

"Yeah, I got it. Why, what's up? You tryna rob him?" Guala inquired ready to rob Shy to get his revenge on for when he robbed him.

"Fuck robbing him we 'bout to try and smoke his lil' ass. Since he did dat snake shit after bein' down here with us all da time. Drop your mask and come on. We gonna try to rear him down," Mello instructed dropping his mask and jogging toward Shy.

Shy was standing at the ice cream truck in front of building 312, talking to Kenny, a light-skinned, pretty girl from up top when the first shot went off.

Boom!

Without looking back or whipping out the Glock 26 Shy took off running up the street toward the alley as fast as he could.

"Man, wtf is that?" KGR and Loc said at the same time whipping out their Glocks and running toward the shots not knowing what to expect.

Mello was jogging, trying to get up on Shy when out of nowhere Guala started shooting before they could get up on him good.

Boom! Boom!

Guala's gun went off recklessly as Shy took off running up the street. Seeing how fast and which way Shy was running Mello stopped chasing, aimed and started shooting hoping to hit him. Out no where, he heard more shots going off. KGR and Loc came out of the alley and saw Shy running like he was Usain Bolt. They saw two masked men standing in the street shooting at him, so they started shooting at them without hesitation. That's when a shootout erupted in the middle of 37th in broad daylight. Mello looked on the other side of the street where Shy, scared as hell, was running. Standing side by side was them two retarded ass young niggas KGR and Loc firing at him and Guala with no remorse.

Boom! Boom! Boom!

As soon as he felt a lil' safe he did what Guala's scared ass was already doing. Ran!

When KGR and Loc saw the two masked men run into the building they already knew who it was.

"Oh, yeah, dem niggas want smoke for real? Bet," Loc said hyped up as they ran off because the police was finally coming.

"Man, why da fuck you start shooting so fast for? We had dat nigga," Mello yelled at Guala, mad that he fucked it up and almost got him hit.

"Man, dat bitch Kenny saw us. So I started hittin'," Guala said still scared as shit as they sat in YaYa's house.

"Well, shit 'bout to get real. We gotta be on point," Mello advised realizing he'd really fucked up.

After the shootout it was hot as shit on 37th, police were everywhere and jumping out every day. As a result of the shootout Kenny got hit in her side, a crackhead got killed who was standing by the buildings and old head Fat Mikey who was standing on 300 hustling got hit twice in his ass while tryna run off.

CHAPTER 6

Two weeks after the heat from the police slowed down Shitty and Squirt were sitting in Shitty's dark blue 300c in front of the alley talking.

"Ay, bra, I bagged your girl's friend last night," Squirt said rolling up some loud.

"Which one cause dem bitches was deep as shit. I ain't even know all dem bitches she brought 'round here." Shitty looked at Squirt.

"Da short, brown-skinned one wit' da long tracks and da blue Victoria Secret sweat suit on. She was phat as shit too in dat joint and she cute," Squirt said

"Yeah, dat's Tierra. I know her. She always wit' my joint dey best friends."

"Dat's what's up. We gotta set dat up den so I can fuck!" Squirt said laughing.

"Say less I got you. But let me ask you sumthin' on some real shit. Do you think I'd be wrong if I rob Turk's scared ass?" Shitty changed the subject.

Squirt looked like he'd just got smacked because he was shocked that Shitty had just asked that. Now if anybody knew how cruddy Shitty is it was Squirt. They go back since they were twelve and thirteen, running around breaking into every house and car they could get in. Plus, they'd caught a situation together. Shitty got locked up, held water and did his time like a man. So, no matter how cruddy he was, he was a loyal and cold-blooded man in Squirt's eyes. That's why what he was taken off a little bit, but not that much now that he thought about it.

"Damn, Bra why you wanna do dat?" Squirt asked confused.

"I mean I know da nigga our cousin. But with him being our blood, he definitely don't act like it. He be too 'noid wen we walk down Double R and dat shit throws me off, kill," Shitty said, trying to get Squirt to see where he was coming from.

"Yeah, but you know dat's just how Turk is. He's a 'noid nigga," Squirt defended.

"Well, I feel like fuck it, since he 'noid for nothin' if I rob him at least he will have sumthin' to be 'noid about."

"You a wild nigga, slim. Kill," Squirt said laughing like shit at Shitty.

"Naw, for real though. Bra I just get bad vibes from dat 'noid nigga," Shitty admitted, laughing but serious at the same time.

"Naw, your ass get money vibes every time you walk down Double R ever since dat sweet ass robbery at da dice game." Shitty was laughing like shit and coughing off the loud.

"No, bullshit they was super sweet. Anyway, fuck dat shit, let me hit my girl and see if her and Tierra together. So, we can link up wit' dem." Shitty pulled out his phone and called Rose his lil' Maryland joint.

"Hello?" Rose answered the phone. She was a redbone, with long black hair. What stood out the most was the tattoo of a large rose on the side of her face, but made her look even better.

"What's up, boo? What you doing?" Shitty asked.

RICO | KINGS OF THE YO

"Nothin'. Coolin' in the house thinking 'bout you. Tierra's ass g'tting' on my nerves. What you doing and where you at anyway?"

"I'm not doin' shit. I'm round my way sittin' in the car wit' Squirt. But look though, since you already wit' Tierra and Squirt's wit' me. I'm 'bout to come get y'all and we can go bowling or out to eat."

"Boy, how you know if Tierrra wanna go out wit, Squirt?"

Tierra snatched the phone from Rose. "Hello, Shitty, what's up, brova?" Teirra said.

"Nothin' coolin' wit, Squirt. We tryna see what's up wit' y'all?" Shitty looked at Squirt.

"Well, why he ain't call my phone?" Tierra questioned with a lil' bass in her voice!

"Hold up, I'ma let you ask," Shitty said, passing Squirt the phone.

"YoYo!" Squirt yelled in the phone soon as he put it to his ear.

"Boy, don't yo-yo me. Why you ain't call or text my phone yet?" Tierra said getting in her feelings.

"My bad, I ain't wanna seem like no stalker and shit we just met last night."

Tierra was out of her feelings now. Yeah, whatever. What's up though what y'all tryna do? Because we bored as shit."

"Shit, it don't matter to me, but I'm hungry as shit. So, we might as well go out to eat somewhere," Squirt suggested feeling on his stomach.

"Your fat ass always hungry," Shitty said.

"Well, a'ight y'all come get us so we can figure out where we going. Just call when y'all get here."

"Say no more." Squirt hung up and gave Shitty his phone back.

"Shit, dat's a bet we gone, bra. Ain't shit out here and it's cold anyway. You got your dog, bra?" Squirt asked Shitty.

Shitty started laughing and put the car in drive. "Dat's like asking is your fat ass gonna eat when we get to the restaurant."

"Fuck you," Squirt said as they pulled off ready to go chill.

As Shitty and Squirt were on their way to try and get some pussy. Turk and Baby Boy was sitting on the side of Turk house down Ridge Road getting money. Turk had Double R pumping like shit, he turned it into a $50 strip and only came out after the rental office closed at 5:00 p.m. One thing nobody could dispute was that no matter how scared Turk was, he knew how to get money. Same thing goes for Baby Boy. I guess that's why they fuck with each other so tough.

"Ay, I'm 'bout to stop being up top and fucking with dem niggas in the Alley," Turk told Baby Boy.

"Damn, why you say dat? What one of dem niggas said sumthin' to you?" Baby Boy responded.

"Naw, but dem niggas be wilding like shit. You know last week Shitty, Flip, Day-Day and Lil E went and shot up every hood dat dey beefing with just because somebody came through that dey ain't know. I watched dese niggas sit around tryna figure out who it could've been Choppa City, Paradise, Simple City, Clay Terrace or Forest Creek. Dese niggas even beefing with Maryland hoods, slim." Turk was talking with his hands, emphasizing his point.

"Yeah, dat's crazy I ain't know dey was beefin' like dat damn."

"Well, dey definitely are. Den when dey couldn't figure it out Shitty gonna say fuck it, let's go through all of dem," Turk said shaking his head.

"Yeah, dat's on dem though. We just go out to the club with dem niggas after dat we can come down here and do us cause when niggas come through dey gonnna go up dere shooting, so we cool," Baby Boy said not really trying to talk about his crew behind their back.

"Oh, and you know dey robbed Zo, too. Dat's some wild shit I would've never called dem niggas if I knew dey was goin do dat to Ziggy. And dem niggas ain't even give me back what I lost."

"Damn, why you ain't ask dem for your shit?" Baby Boy looked at Turk like he was stupid as shit for setting up a lick and not even getting his money back.

"Man, I told Squirt when I saw him and Flip down bottom. And guess what his fat ass gonna say?"

"What?" Baby Boy looked at Turk smiling knowing Squirt.

"He gonna tell me they split everything up. So, I said shit I thought I was supposed to be part of dat split? Den he gonna tell me next time don't think because dat's not my strong suit."

Baby Boy was laughing like shit, but mad at the same time at how they carried his man. "Man, you gotta accept dat. Because you know dem niggas fifty-fifty. Dey only play fair with each other and dey probably don't even do dat knowing dem."

"It's cool cause I'm just gonna start keeping my distance that's all."

"Well, I'm 'bout to see who tryna go out. Let me see your car so I can ride up there right quick. You tryna go to the C.F.E or Tradewinds?" Turk said, handing him his car keys to his egg white 2010 Lincoln LS.

"Man, we going to the C.F.E. to fuck with TCB. A'ight I'ma 'bout to hop in the shower. I'ma walk up there later," Turk said going in the house to get ready for the GoGo.

* * * * * *

Two Hours Later

The alley was packed with niggas waiting to go to the club. Mack, Turk, Bo, Eroc, Zo, Lil E, Flip, Lips, Sway, Day-Day, Shy, Baby Boy, Loc and KGR were going out. The CFE on Saturday was for people eighteen and over but that shit didn't matter because as long as you had money and clout you could be ten-years-old and still get in and 37th definitely had both. They had been regulars in the GoGo's since Hot Boy and Mad-Chef days. Everybody in the alley was laughing, smoking, drinking, and of course fly as shit. They all had on Burberry, Versace or Hugo Boss and New Balance, Nike, Prada or Foamposite shoes. It's crazy how they came together to go out no matter what was going on with them individually. All that shit went out the window when it came time to hit the club.

"Ay, where the fuck Squirt and Shitty at? I know dey tryna go out," Day-Day said to Lil' E who was drinking a bottle of Rose Moet.

"Shit, I don't know I can't fit dem niggas in my pockets with all dis money, especially Squirt's fat ass," Lil E said causing everybody to burst out laughing.

"Dem niggas been together since earlier. I saw dem pull off in Shitty's 300," Flip said.

"A'ight, bet. Fuck it y'all ready to roll out den?" Day-Day asked everybody.

"Yeah, how many dogs we taking? Because y'all know we might get into it," Lips said to everybody.

"I got Squirt's Camaro, Turk's driving, Mac driving, and you so we mines well put one in each car, dat should be cool," Flip said to Lips.

"A'ight, bet," Lil' E said to Mac.

"Lil E ride with me, bra. We gone, y'all," Lip said as everybody started going to the cars.

The CFE was off Marlboro Pike behind the Marlo Furniture Store on the Maryland side in a lil' shopping center. It was a big spot and it stayed packed, tonight was no different. They pulled in the parking lot and after riding around, they eventually parked within close distant of each other. As they got close to the club, they could see that the line was long as shit! But that never mattered to them because 37th was definitely going through the cut-line. Only Maryland niggas and broke niggas waited in line, oh, and of course bitches. As soon as they walked up bitches were on their dicks and niggas were hatin' like shit as usual.

"Damn, bitch look at that lil' ass boy they got with them. He can't be over twelve? But damn he looks good with dem long ass dreads," some random broad waiting in line said talking to her friends about Loc.

"You heard what shawdy said, Loc?" Shy asked.

"Yeah, I heard her. Come on we 'bout to bag dem bitches and purp at the same time. Hold up, y'all," Loc told everybody. Him, Shy and KGR went to holla at the broad and her friends. "What's up wit', y'all?" Loc said to the brown-skinned one who made the comment.

She was bad is shit, she was 5'7, with a baby face and a nice body. She was with five other girls who also looked good.

"Aww, I ain't know you heard me," she said embarrassed.

"Yeah, I heard you. And if you was ugly I would've purped, but since you bad. You and all your friends ain't gotta stand out here in da cold no more because y'all coming with us. So, tell dem to tell you thank you." Loc smiled.

"Boy, do you know how much dat's gonna cost to get all six of us through the cut-line?" She still looked at Loc as a lil boy, but that was about to change.

"Naw, I don't know how much it cost because I know whatever it is I can cover it. I might be young in age, but my pockets older than your grandfather. So, y'all coming or what? Cause we gone," Loc said as Shy and KGR started walking toward the door.

"Hell yeah, we coming wit' your cute ass," she said, walking behind Loc and the rest of the 37th niggas.

After they were searched they went into the club and had a ball all night.

CHAPTER 7

The next day Squirt and Shitty were outside in the alley early in the morning, chilling and talking 'bout last night.

"Ay, slim, Tierra pussy a torch," Squirt said smiling hard as shit.

"Oh, yeah? She definitely was on you hard as shit she better have gave you some pussy," Shitty said.

"No bullshit, but for real though she cool as shit. I fuck with her personality. Anyway, did you talk to Day-Day or one of dem niggas yet?" Squirt asked pulling out his phone.

"Yeah, I hollered at Loc. Him and KGR 'bout to pull up. Dey went to White Corners to grab sumthin' to eat," Shitty said talking about a historic breakfast spot at the top of the hill next to the Hobo Shop that hustlers all over the city went to eat and bullshit around.

"Damn, why you ain't tell dem niggas to get us nothin' to eat? You know I'm hungry as shit," Squirt said smiling.

"Nah," Shitty said, shaking head.

"What's up with y'all?" KGR said, bending the corner into the alley with a bag.

"Shit cooling. One of y'all got some loud?" Shitty asked as Loc hit the alley with a bag too.

"Yeah, I got some, bra. You gotta roll up cause I'm 'bout to eat," Loc said, handing Shitty the loud and backwoods.

55

"Damn, y'all petty asses ain't bring a nigga nothin' to eat? Fuck that weed." Squirt looked at their bags.

Loc and KGR both bust out laughing.

"I told you this fat ass was gonna want something."

"Here, take the bag," KGR said to Loc, handing Squirt the bag with his food in it.

"Good lookin', bra. I hope this shit pork cause I ain't with that wack shit," Squirt said as they all burst out laughing and started eating and chilling talking 'bout their night.

● ● ● ● ● ●

Later That Night

"Duck down, Moe! Bra, duck da fuck down!" Loc yelled at KGR.

They were in the back of a gay girl's house named Keda. Keda was a twenty-seven-year old tomboy with dreads and a little chubby. Keda acted like and hung with men, she was known to get money and loved to gamble all day. She regularly went to the alley and messed with Shitty and his crew with the dice. She rarely lost because her money was so long, but they fucked with her because she was cool and about her money.

"Moe, Ms. Joann gonna see your wild ass," Loc said to KGR referring to Keda's mother.

"Man, no she ain't. And I don't even think Keda's gay ass in dere." They were at the back window of Keda's house waiting to see if they saw her inside to rob her.

"Bra, it's two in the morning. I know her fat ass in dere. I'm just 'bout to knock on the door, and make her come out," Loc said, getting frustrated like they'd been waiting for hours, when they actually only been there less than ten minutes.

56

"Bra, how da fuck you gonna make her come out? It's two in the fucking morning," KGR stated.

Loc looked at him like he was crazy. "I'ma tell her shitty said come to da alley, it's a big crap game over dere. Her fat ass gonna be geeked and gonna bring a bag wit' her," Loc said, laughing like using his brother's name for some shit like this was nothing.

"Bra, you better not use Shitty's name. He's gonna fuck you up," KGR said with all seriousness.

"Bra, I don't care. Dat's da only way we gonna get her out here. And I'ma give him some of da money," Loc said as he started knocking on the door without a second thought.

After the first three knocks Ms. Joeann answered. "Hey, Lil' Malik? What y'all want it's two sumthin' in da damn morning."

"Is Keda in dere? If so, tell her my brova Shitty said come to da alley asap. Dey gamblin' good shooting fifties and dey sweet."

"A'ight, I'ma go tell her now. Y'all lil' asses need to be in da house somewhere," Ms. Joann said as she closed her door in their faces without waiting for a reply.

"Ugly, old, bitch," Loc said as soon as the door shut.

"Man, do you think dat shit gonna work? And get her fat ass out here?" KGR said as they started walking off.

"Hell yeah!" Loc yelled as he stopped walking.

"Look," he said, pointing behind them.

Keda was coming out of her back door in a rush putting on a red and black Gucci sweater.

"Ay, lil' Malik. Hold up, y'all!" Keda yelled to them jogging, trying to catch up with them.

"What's up wit' y'all?" Keda said as she got up on them and gave them dap.

"Shit coolin'!" They both yelled at the same time.

57

"Where the fuck your brova and dem at gambling? I had to rush out here for dat sweet money," Keda said to Loc smiling.

"Dey was in da alley, but dey just took da crap game down bottom in the building," Loc said keeping his lie going and eyeing Keda's pockets.

"We 'bout to walk down dere now," KGR said to Keda giving Loc a little assistance.

"Shid, come on," Keda replied, pulling money out of her pockets as she walked counting out at least ten-thousand dollars in all hundreds, and fifties.

Loc's eyes almost popped out of his head when he saw how much money Keda pulled out of her pockets. Loc knew Keda was going to bring out a bag, but he never thought it was going to be as much as he was seeing now. It had him and KGR drooling, if she had only brought out a thousand dollars it would've been a plus for them as they acted like they was headed down bottom KGR whipped out his Glock 17 and slapped Keda in the back of her head. Keda stumbled forward before catching her balance, but dropped all her money out of her hand.

"What's goin' on y'all?" Keda said as she looked up with fear in her eyes.

KGR grabbed her by the collar of her Gucci sweater with his Glock pointed at her head. "Bitch, shut the fuck up. You know what it is?" Loc said, looking at her while he got on his knees and started picking up all the money she dropped on the ground.

"Lil' Malik I seen you grow up, shorty. Y'all gonna do dis to me?" Keda said with tears in her eyes now.

"Didn't he tell you to shut the fuck up, bitch!" KGR yelled as he slapped her with his Glock three more times in the face. Keda grabbed her face that was now dripping with blood as KGR threw her to the ground and kicked her in her stomach.

"See I told your fat ass to shut up. Now look at you," Loc said smiling. "I should smoke your ass for making me pick up all dis motherfuckin' money off da ground," Loc continued pointing his Ruger P.91 down at Keda after picking the money up off the ground.

"Please, Lil' Malik, you ain't got to shoot me. Dat money ain't 'bout shit. Pleaseeee," Keda begged Loc knowing from the story she'd heard about Loc he'd most definitely shoot her.

"What you think, bra?" Loc asked KGR.

"Bra, fuck dis bitch. Ain't no need to kill her. We got da money, we gone," KGR said as he started running off.

"Ay, good lookin', Keda. We bout to go find us a crap game. Hopefully we find sumthin' sweet," Loc said laughing.

"Moe, wait you scared ass nigga!" Loc yelled at KGR as he ran off trying catch up with his right-hand man.

CHAPTER 8

"How many you tryna get?" Squirt asked a crackhead who'd just walked up looking for drugs.

Squirt, Baby Boy and Lil E were in the alley doing their usual smoking loud, selling drugs and talking shit.

"I want three for fifty, Boo-Boo. But is dey big?" the crackhead said not wanting no small bad crack for her fifty dollars.

"Man, yeah! You want 'em or not? You always do dat shit so you can pick through a nigga's shit. You not 'bout to pick through my shit today. I ain't got time for dat shit. You can take your money somewhere else for all dat," Squirt fussed at the crackhead.

"Boo-Boo, don't do dat. Dis my last fifty. I'm just tryna make sure I'm straight all day. But I'm not gonna pick through em, just give me three nice ones, Boo-Boo," the crackhead replied mad that she couldn't pick the rocks she wanted.

"Here," Squirt said, handing the crackhead three nice size bags of crack.

"Dese ain't dat big, but dey a'ight looking. I'll take em though, Boo-Boo." The crackhead looked at the bag of crack in her hand and handed Squirt $50, then walked off.

"Man, crackhead Angel be in da way, don't she, bra?" Lil E said to Squirt laughing after Squirt walked back up from putting away his stash.

"Kill, Moe! Dat bitch be doing too much sometimes for real," Squirt agreed shaking his head.

"Baby Boy, what the fuck is up?" Squirt asked Baby Boy who was in deep thought.

"Man, I been out here all day tryna run my bag up and its slow as shit. I gotta find a move or sumthin' cause my girl 'bout to have the baby next month and everything," Baby Boy complained.

"Yeah, I'm already hip. You most definitely gotta run up a bag or hit a lick. Dem baby's will bust your ass, Kill," Squirt replied laughing.

"Ay, who da fuck is dat right dere, y'all?" Lil E asked Squirt and Baby Boy. It was a brown-skinned dude about 5'9, two-hundred pounds even, with a low haircut, a temp on the sides and a long beard, wearing a dark blue Helly Hanson coat, walking toward them with his had behind his back like he was hiding something.

Squirt called out to him, "Ay, who the fuck dat?" Squirt yelled to the unknown man gripping the handle of his Glock 30 in it through his shirt without whipping it out.

The unknown man just looked up at Squirt but never stop walking toward them. Suddenly the unknown man stopped for a brief second and locked eyes with Squirt. Squirt was trying hard to put a name to the man's face, but couldn't come up with nothing, when out of the blue the unknown man came from behind his back with a black and grey Taurus 45 and without hesitation started firing at them.

Bop! Bop! Bop! Bop! Bop! Bop!

The unknown man fired furiously now becoming the unknown shooter.

61

"Man, watch out!" Squirt said to Lil E and Baby Boy as he whipped out his Glock 30 and begin returning fire.

Bok! Bok! Bok! Bok!

Squirt fired as he ran behind the dumpster that sat in the back of the alley for cover. Lil' E pulled out his Glock 27 and begin firing at the unknown shooter as well.

Blocka! Blocka! Blocka! Blocka! Blocka! Blocka!

Lil' E fired six shots from his Glock which made the unknown shooter back up a little bit, but never flinch and kept firing Taurus.

Bop! Bop! Bop! Bop! Bop!

As the unknown shooter kept firing Baby Boy tried to run up the steps to grab his gun dat he had stashed, as he did, he opened himself up catching three shots to his back and one to his neck. When Squirt saw Baby Boy get hit, out of anger he came from behind the dumpster firing recklessly.

Bok! Bok! Bok! Bok! Bok! Bok! Bok! Bok! Bok!

As Squirt came out shooting, he almost caught a bullet to the face, which grazed him when the unknown shooter saw dat, Squirt grabbed his face and ran back behind the dumpster. He thought he'd hit him. So with that being his goal to come and shoot Squirt or Shitty if he was outside, he exchanged a couple more shots in ow mowtion for a brief second before running back the way he came from to an awaiting car and disappeared.

"Man, who da fuck was dat?" Lil E yelled to Squirt who was feeling his face with one hand, while holding his Glock in the other.

"Man, I don't know! But Slim looked familiar. But fuck dat right now. Baby Boy hit bad. I saw him get hit in his neck and back. I'm 'bout to go get the car. Go pick him up! We gotta take him to the hospital because he gonna bleed out by the time the ambulance comes!" Squirt yelled as he ran off to get the car.

Squirt pulled back up in less than two minutes in his Camaro. He jumped out and helped Lil' E put Baby Boy in the backseat of the car and they jumped back in and pulled off headed to Greater Southeast Hospital.

While Squirt and Lil E was taking Baby Boy to the hospital, Shitty, Day-Day, and Flip were on the other side of the city in a hood called Congress Park to be exact trying to strike gold. Flip had gotten a call from a little bitch he'd been fucking that one of their main vicks they was beefin' with was 'bout to leave one of her girlfriend's house. Their vick's name was Tario and he was from a hood called Simple City that they'd been beefin' with for years. Tario was a real shooter and they'd been trying to get at him for years, but never had luck due to him always being on point and staying strap with a gun ready to shoot. Their beef started three years ago when Tario shot Squirt's brother KGR in his leg for disrespecting him, KGR was just fourteen at the time.

Tario is light-skinned, 5'7, one-hundred and sixty pounds, with a Caesar haircut and as ruthless as they come.

"Ay, Moe, we just on time dat nigga still in dere. Dat's da house right dere," Flip said to Shitty and Day-Day who was in a stolen dark green Jeep 2004 Liberty with tinted windows that they'd parked behind a red 2008 Cadillac CTS.

"Bet! I'm about to flush him when he comes out. I been geekin' to kill his scary ass for a brick, Kill," Shitty said, gripping the thirteen shot P.90 Ruger that he'd taken from Guala weeks ago.

"Man, dere he go right dere!" Day-Day yelled to Shtty getting excited.

63

Tario was coming out of the front door across the street heading right in their direction. He was wearing a blue and grey Hugo Boss sweat suit, and some Balenciaga's, talking on his cell phone not sensing the danger he was in.

"Moe, I think he's drivin' dis CTS in front of us," Shitty said with his hands on the door ready to jump out on their vick.

"He is, bruh," Flip said excitedly seeing the Cadillac CTS lights blink when Tario pointed his right hand in the car's direction. That's when they noticed that he had the remote to the alarm in his hand.

"He just hit the unlock button. Don't jump out bra wait until he gets in the car. I'ma box him in," Flip said to Shitty who still had his right hand on the door getting ready to jump out.

"Ay everybody get all way down in case he looks dis way. Here he comes now," Day-Day said and everybody got low.

Tario walked straight up to the red Cadillac CTS and jump in. As soon as he closed the door, Flip pulled right up on the side of him and box him in his parking spot.

"What's up, big boy?" Shitty said, looking Tario in the face coming out of his window with his Ruger.

Tario froze like he'd seen a ghost when he saw Shitty's face.

Bok! Bok! Bok! Bok! Bok! Bok! Shitty fired into the window of Tario's CTS shattering the driver's side window and catching him in his face and chest multiple times before jumping out of the car. Once out the car Shitty with his Ruger in his right hand grabbed Tario, who was dying, but still breathing by the neck of his bloody Hugo Boss sweater through the window with his left hand and gave him six more shots all in his head then jumped back in the car.

"Dat was all of dem," Shitty said, smiling and taking the clip out of his Ruger showing it to Flip and Day-Day.

"Your shit burn," Day-Day said to Shitty.

They all started laughing as Flip pulled off heading back around the Yo.

CHAPTER 9

The very next day after Baby Boy got shot Shitty, Squirt and Shy happened to see Leeky as they were driving up Minnesota Avenue located in Northeast heading to their hood. Shitty had just came from pickin' up Squirt from his house and Shy from over a little bitch's house.

"Oh, yeah, bra y'all see dat nigga Leeky lackin' like dat!" Shy yelled to Shitty and Squirt from the back seat of the car after just spotting Leeky entering the liquor store on Minnesota Ave right across the street from the McDonalds.

"Yeah, I see his scared ass," Squirt said laughing.

"Ay Shitty pull over in the liquor store parking lot, bra. I see his car parked right dere," Shy said.

"A'ight," Shitty said making a left in the parking lot, parking two cars down from Leeky's silver 2019 Dodge Charger.

"So, what y'all gonna do?" Shy yelled to Shitty and Squirt soon as Shitty put the car in park.

"*What we gonna do?* Nigga what the fuck you gonna do? Dem niggas hit at you!" Squirt yelled back to Shy who had a dumb look on his face, why Shitty busted out laughing.

"Man, I'll hit him. I don't fuck wit' dat nigga anyway," Shitty said, grabbing his Mac-10 from under his seat.

"Nah, Shitty let bra do it. He spotted him out like he wanted some work, let him work," Squirt advised.

"Man, I ain't duckin' nothin', I'll do it!" Shy yelled.

"Y'all must think I keep dis glizzy on me for nothin'?" Shy continued as he pulled out his Glock 26.

"Dere he go right dere!" Shitty yelled, geekin to see Shy finally put in some work.

Leeky was coming from around the corner from the liquor store heading to his car with a bottle of Patron in his hand.

"Nah, bra, wait till he gets in the car so he can't try to get outta dere," Squirt said to Shy stopping him from jumping out the car door.

Shitty and Squirt both yelled, "Go!"

Shy jumped out the backseat, glizzy in hand, heading to handle his business. As soon as Leeky shut his car door Shy was right up on him.

"Damn, Leeky, what's up?" Shy said as he got up on him with his Glock pointed at his face being sarcastic.

"Hold, Shy, what the fuck is up, Moe?" Leeky yelled as he rolled his window down surprised and shocked that Shy was standing in front of him with a Glock in his face, which just happened to be the same Glock they took from him weeks ago.

"What the fuck it look like? I'm 'bout to make you eat dis glizzy," Shy said pulling the trigger.

Bok! Bok! Bok! Bok! Bok!

He hit Leeeky all in his face.

"And let me get dis patron. You ain't gonna need it where you goin," Shy said as he opened Leeky's car door and grabbed the bottle of liquor he'd just bought.

"Come the fuck on!" Squirt yelled to Shy as he and Shitty pulled up behind Leeky car.

"Man, I was gettin' us a bottle!" Shy yelled back at Squirt as he ran and got in the car.

"Fuck dat bottle, bra. You should've went in dat nigga's pockets," Shitty said to Shy as he pulled off heading back around the Yo.

* * * * * *

Two Hours Later

Down bottom Mello, Fat Marcus, Eroc, Croc and Guala were in YaYa's house just cooling, smokin', waiting for weed sells and playing 2k20 basketball on X-box One when they found out the news of Leeky being killed down Minnesota Ave. YaYa came in the house loud as shit, crying and barely able to talk with the news.

YaYa was a thirty-one-years old, fat, brown-skinned woman that reminded you of Monique off the tv show The Parkers. YaYa was Shitty's cousin and Croc's girlfriend, her house was slightly the trap down bottom.

"Ay, Moe, somebody killed Leeky at da liquor store!" YaYa yelled, slamming the door and out of breath.

"What!" Mello and Fat Marcus said at the same time shocked by what they were hearing.

Eroc, Croc and Guala just had blank looks on their faces.

"Yeah, Moe, somebody killed him down Minnesota on da side of the liquor store in the parking lot," YaYa repeated trying to calm herself down.

"His lil' brova Guggi just was out front cryin' and everything. He said he got hit all in his face," YaYa continued as she started crying again thinking about how Leeky got killed.

"Damn, Moe, dat's why dat nigga been gone for like two and a half hours," Fat Marcus said shaking his head.

"Fuck! We got to go see what the fuck happen!" Mello yelled as he got up and headed out the door heated, everybody followed him, but YaYa.

Outside of YaYa's building was live. It seemed like everybody that was from 37th was down there, due to Leeky getting killed. Mello, Fat Marcus and Guala were standing on the building front asking everybody that walked had they seen Leeky's lil' brother Guggi so they could see what he knew about his brother being killed, but hadn't nobody seen him.

"Man, Guggi lil' ugly ass probably wit' his family and shit right now," Fat Marcus said to Mello and Guala.

"Nah, for real, cause dat's where I'd be if I wasn't around the way and my brova got killed," Guala said agreeing with Fat Marcus.

"Yeah, I'm already hip. But who y'all think did dat shit?" Mello said, lookng at Fat Marcus and Guala trying to see if they had an idea.

"Man, he got killed down da Ave, Sir. Anybody could've did dat shit. Slim niggas beefing wit' a hunnid niggas, it's almost impossible to figure out who hit, bra," Fat Marcus said shaking his head making sense of the whole situation.

"Nah dat's law, dis shit crazy. And we slightly beefin' wit' da alley and dem niggas could've did dat shit but I doubt it. Cause dem niggas ain't even come down here shooting yet. Dey probably don't even know dat was us dat hit at Shy since we had masks on. Guala said to Mello.

"Dem niggas know we did dat shit. Dem niggas just be on some snaky shit, but I don't think dey killed Leeky. If dey did, it's gonna come to da light sooner or later and shit gonna get real," Mello said to Guala and Fat Marcus heading to Leeky's mother's house to see what his family heard about his murder.

CHAPTER 10

A Week Later

Day-Day, Lil E and Flip were over Day-Day's aunt's house around a hood called Edgewood, just chillin, talkin' shit and laying low like always when 37th was hot with police. They'd been laying low over there since Baby Boy got shot in da alley a couple of days ago which had the police posted there. Day-Day, Lil E, Flip, and a friend of theirs from Edgewood named, S. Dot were smoking trying to figure out who it was that shot Baby Boy.

"Dey said dem people still in the alley parked," Flip said to Day-Day and Lil E, talkin' 'bout the police still around 37th.

"Who was dat?" Lil E asked Flip wondering who he was talkin' to on the phone.

"Dat was Turk," Flip said, puttin' his phone in his pocket.

"Why da fuck you lookin' all zone out?" Flip asked Day-Day who was daydreaming.

"Nah, I'm just wondering who the fuck shot my brother," Day-Day said still in deep thought.

"Y'all don't know who the fuck y'all beefin' wit'?" S. Dot asked, looking at everybody.

RICO | KINGS OF THE YO

"Y'all said he ain't have no face mask on when he walked up. Baby Boy or Shitty ain't recognize da nigga?" S. Dot continued.

"Nah, Albert Einstein. Don't you think we would fuckin' know who it was by now!" Lil E yelled at S. Dot.

"Yeah, you right," S. Dot replied.

"Dat's crazy we don't no who dat was. Shitty said soon as he saw dat nigga they locked eyes and the nigga just start hittin'. But he said he's never seen slim before," Day-Day said getting mad.

"Dat could've been a hit from anybody. We beefin' wit' like five different hoods and dem niggas fuck wit' a lot of people. It could've been a favor for a favor. Dat's what niggas doing now," Flip said making a lot of sense. "When they can't get up on you themselves because you know them. They'll get somebody you don't know to get at you and they will do the same favor for them, that's why they call it a favor for a favor."

"No bullshit. You most definitely right, bra," Day-Day said to Flip standing up from the couch. "What happens in the dark always comes to light. I'm 'bout to go back around to the Yo' and get up on Shitty and Squirt to see what dey heard. I'm 'bout to just start goin' around different hoods we beef wit' smokin shit," Day-Day swore to Flip and Lil E as he headed to the door wit' them on his heels.

"You know I'm wit it," Lil' E said as they left to head back around 37th.

Three Hours Later

Day-Day, Shitty, Loc, KGR, Squirt and Lips were all chilling in the alley since the heat had died down from the shootout. They all were strapped and geeking for some smoke except Lips.

"Man, y'all niggas need to squash that shit with down bottom," Lips said to all of them.

"Nigga you talkin' 'bout squash sumthin' after dem niggas tried to smoke Shy? Fuck is wrong wit' you?" KGR replied mad that Lips was tryna cop.

"Yeah, but y'all niggas started it by robbing dem for their dogs and den y'all going whip out on Mello. Y'all know he wasn't gonna just take dat on the chin. And Squirt you a wild nigga cause Mello your man you were supposed to stop dat shit before it got dat far," Lips chastised Squirt.

"Fuck you, nigga! I brought him up here tryna dead it before it went somewhere else but that nigga start talking 'bout smacking niggas so that's on him. Then this nigga gonna try to get up on Shy so he crossed the line," Squirt said looking at Lip.

"I feel you slim, but y'all taking up for Shy scared ass when he ain't even shoot back for himself and he ain't get hit so that hit can still be squashed before blood gets drawn." Lips tried to reason with the youngins before shit got too ugly. Not knowing that blood had already been drawn and they were responsible for Leeky being killed.

"Man, Squirt, Mello's your man so you can holla at him and see wat he tryna do. But if he purp we gonna start fucking down bottom up nonstop," Day-Day promised giving Squirt an out because he knew he really ain't wanna beef with Mello because that was his man, but his loyalty to alley boys made him choose sides.

"Bet I'ma holla at him later on before shit gets outta hand," Squirt said to Day-Day happy that he ain't have to beef with his man.

As soon as they got finished talking 'bout that Zo black walked up. "What's up with y'all, baby? Zo dapped everybody up as if they ain't never rob him.

"Ziggy, fuck you coming from?" Shitty asked Zo.

"I just came from down Double R with Turk and Baby Boy. Dat joint doin' numbers down dere," Zo said talking about how much money they was getting down Ridge Road.

"Oh, yeah?" Shitty asked while catching Squirt eyes.

"Hell yeah, and I could've caught some sells, if I had some coke, but Fatz ain't fuckin' wit' me since y'all robbed me for his money," Zo said making everybody laugh at how nonchalant he was about getting robbed.

"Fuck Fatz scared ass and nigga I told you to leave, but you had a S on your chest," Squirt reminded Zo.

"But Fatback Kane, I couldn't leave my brova. I had to at least try to take him, but if I would've known his ass ain't even have that much money on him I would've left his ass," Zo said and everybody burst out laughing.

"Your ass retarded, slim. Ay, but seriously, how much you have on you when dat shit happened?" Shitty asked reaching in his pockets.

"Thirty five hundred," Zo said fast as shit.

"Nigga stop lying! Your 'noid ass ain't walking around with that much money on you," Shitty said about to say fuck it since Zo tried to lie.

"I had to try, Shitty. But for real I had fourteen hundred and eighty dubs of coke on me dat Lil E dirty ass took out of my socks," Zo said making everybody laugh again.

"Here go a stack, slim. But I ain't got no coke for you and da only reason I'm doing dis is because I fuck with you," Shitty said handing Zo a $1000.

"Hit my phone in like an hour, Ziggy. I'ma give you a deuce of coke and you just owe me for a thirty-one a'ight," Squirt said.

"Oh, y'all dirty asses must finally got some pussy? Cause y'all being nice as shit," Zo said, causing niggas to laugh.

"Naw, niggas just fuck wit' you. So, we lookin' out cause dat shit wasn't supposed to happen like dat with you," Shitty said.

"Shiddd, y'all niggas could rob me more often if dat's the case," Zo said, laughing and making everybody else laugh hard as shit.

"Man, you burnt out, Ziggy, but for real hit my phone in an hour and I got you. Oh, and fuck Fatz, sir holla at me when you need something," Squirt said dappin' up Zo.

"A'ight Fatback Kane, I'ma hit you later and I'ma holla at the rest of y'all later," Zo said then walked off.

It was 11 p.m., Flip, Squirt and Shitty were down Stoneridge waiting for Mello to meet them across from his baby mother's building. Squirt had called Flip and let him know that he was trying get the beef squashed between the alley and down bottom. Flip was all for it because he was stuck in the middle and eventually, he would have to choose sides.

"What's up with y'all?" Mello said, walking up with his hand on his dog which was poking out because of the 30 clip.

"Damn, bra, you coming down here gripping like I would bring you a move," Flip said in his feeling by Mello thinking he might set him up.

"Flip, I don't know what to think, but I gave you the benefit of the doubt because if not, I would've came shooting," Mello said not ducking nothing still.

"See you still purping dat's how dis shit got started. A nigga know you ain't no bitch. But neither are we and da difference is all us gonna work in da alley. You da only one gonna work down bottom and you know dat. Dem scared niggas ain't tryna beef. Da only reason we ain't mash the gas on dis shit yet is on da strength of you and Squirt's relationship. But if you keep purpin' all dat shit gonna go out da window and we gonna run through dat down bottom shit like at Mac Truck," Shitty said with venom, gripping his Glock. 30 he had on him and looking at Mello in his eyes.

Sensing shit was 'bout to get ugly Squirt stepped up and spoke, "Look fuck all that shit. All dat shit is dead, what happened, happened. Ain't no changin' dat shit so we pass dat. Let's squash dis shit before blood gets drawn because we know ain't no comin' back after dat," Squirt advised Shitty and Mello.

"I feel where y'all comin' from but y'all know I fucked with Leeky and I fuck with Guala. So, I had to come say sumthin' 'bout y'all robbing dem. Y'all would've done the same if I would've bagged one of y'all scared men," Mello said calming down now.

"Yeah, you definitely supposed to do dat. But it's how you do it, slim. You know you can't disrespect a man and say you gonna smack somebody, cause dat's taking shit to another level," Shitty explained.

"I respect dat cuz and dat's my bad. Look, Leeky's dead now, but let Guala get his dog back for me cuz." Mello told Shitty trying get at least one gun back out of the situation.

"I can't do dat, slim. You know I ain't givin' no dog back. And I already did my good deed and charity for the year," Shitty said laughing, talking about what he did for Zo earlier.

"Damn, you know dat's my man, though," Mello said to Shitty shaking his head giving up on getting Guala's gun back.

"Yeah, I'm already sharp. But he brought dat on himself by throwing the alley on Leeky and dat shit backfired. So, dat's on him," Shitty stated.

"What?" Mello was completely confused.

"I can see dat your man left you in the blind. So, I'ma put you on point. Guala, hit my phone and told me Leeky had the dog on him. He kept him right dere till we got down there because he thought I was gonna give him the Smith. 40 dat I was tryna swap with Leeky, if he helped me snake him out of the Glizzy." Shitty switched it up a little giving Mello the majority of the truth.

Everything started making sense to Mello now. "Damn, that nigga Leeky did say he was 'bout to go in YaYa's house, but Guala told him to wait until he sold some more coke," Mello said now seeing the play Guala put on Leeky

"Yeah, that nigga's a snake. So, we snaked his ass, too. Fuck him, but at least he could've put you on point since you gonna be da one who goes to war for him." Shitty really tried to get in Mello's head.

"Dat bitch ass nigga got all dis shit started cause he on some snake shit. Don't even trip I got something for him. As far as dat shit with us, dat shit's dead. Tell Shy fat ass I said my bad," Mello said mad, but laughing at his last words like everybody else was.

"No question that shit dead and everything love, slim." Shitty dapped Mello up. "A'ight, bra hit my phone later."

"Oh, I'm definitely gonna hit your phone cause I'ma have a play y'all going love," Mello said with a smirk on his face.

CHAPTER 11

"Rico, where you 'bout to go?" Shitty's sister Dime asked, calling him by his real name as he was tucking his Glock 30 in his pants before putting his throbe on over top of his outfit.

Shitty was over his mother's house getting dress to go to Jumah which is mandatory for all Muslim on Friday. Dime was Shitty, Lil E and Loc's sister and the only one who still lived with their mother. Dime at seventeen was three years younger than Shitty, a year younger than Lil E and a year older than Loc. She was by far the baddest young bitch around 37th. Dime was small at 5'3', dark-skinned, one-hundred and twenty-five pounds. She was Shitty, Lil E and Loc's only sister and their heart.

"Diamond, sometimes I think you just be wanting to get on a nigga nerves. You see I'm putting on my throbe where else am I going?" Shitty said, calling Dime by her real name as well. Shaking his head he grabbed his car keys.

"Oh, you 'bout to go to Jumah? It is Friday, huh?" Dime said smiling.

"Girl you so smart you should've been a lawyer," Shitty joked. "You figure it all out by yourself," Shitty continued.

"Boy, shut up," Dime said, laughing and hitting Shitty in his chest with three punches.

"Girl, stop playing I'm 'bout to leave," Shitty said playfully running past his sister to the front door to leave.

"A'ight give me fifty dollars," Dime requested with her hand out.

"Damn, dat's all you do is beg," Shitty joked handing her a $100 bill.

"Thanks, bruh!" Dime smiled as she grabbed the money and kissed Shitty on the cheek.

"I'ma see you later," Shitty said as he opened the front door.

"A'ight," Dime said as he left.

* * * * * *

Twenty Minutes Later

Shitty was at Jumah in Capitol Height, Maryland which was called The Islamic Research Center with Shy and Turk who he happened to see riding up Ridge Road on his way to Jumah.

"Where da fuck is Loc and Sway? Dey ain't going to Jumah?" Turk said as they exited the car getting ready to go in the Jumah.

"Who knows where Loc at and Sway went to Jumah down 46th with Jake, Spunk and 'em," Shitty said, fixing his throbe making sure his gun print couldn't be seen.

"Man, I don't trust dem niggas," Turk said of Jake and Spunk wit' a frown on his face.

"Dey ain't for you to trust. We be fuckin' wit' dem you don't. So, you should be a'ight," Shitty said, looking at Turk.

"I'm just sayin," Turk said, lookin' at Shitty still goin on about Jake and Spunk. "Dem niggas snakes," he continued, shaking his head.

"Look, man, I'm not tryna hear dat scared ass shit right now! You don't fuck wit' em, and dey don't fuck wit' you. So, it is what it is. I'm 'bout to go in dis Masjid," Shitty said, brushing off Turk's comment and entering the Jumah service with Shy followed with Turk not far behind.

❋ ❋ ❋ ❋ ❋ ❋

After the Jumah service Shitty, Shy, and Turk was heading to Shitty's 300c to go back around their hood when Shitty spotted a dude he knew form Barry Farms a neighborhood that sits in the heart of Southeast Washington, D.C.

He was headed toward him and calling his name, "Ay, Shitty! Hold fast."

Shitty, Shy and Turk stopped. "As Salam Alaykum," Shitty said as the dude came in arm's reach.

They embraced and gave each other dap and a hug.

"Walakum Salaam," the dude returned the greeting.

The dude's name was Fat Dobey. Shitty met Fat Dobey over DC jail, the JUV Block when Shitty was fighting a body he'd beat three years ago. Fat Dobey was a fat boy, dark-brown-skinned, 5'6, and two-hundred and twenty pounds, with dreadlocks that hang to his stomach.

Fat Dobey was always on some bullshit or knew about some bullshit, that's why Shitty kicked it with him.

"Wat da fuck is up? I ain't seen you in a minute, bra?" Fat Dobey said with a slur as he spoke with his tongue.

"I been coolin' stayin' out da way," Shitty said.

"Yeah, I been on da same shit for real. I'm tryna start fuckin' wit' dat rap shit," Fat Dobey said.

"Yeah, ain't nothing wrong wit dat. But my man right here da best in da city wit' dat rap shit." Shitty pointed at Shy.

"Nah, I'm da boss in dat rap shit for real," Fat Dobey challenged smiling but was dead serious.

"Stop what you doing," Shy said as him, Turk, and Shitty started laughing.

"Nah for real. But anyway, I got some info you can use Shitty. Holla at me one on one right quick," Fat Dobey said seriously as he and Shitty walked off by themselves, getting out of Shy and Turk's ears reach so they couldn't hear the conversation.

"What's up, bra?" Shitty said soon as they were away from Shy and Turk.

"Wasn't you in a shootout around your way like a week ago and your man got hit?" Fat Dobey asked serious.

"Yeah. Why, what's up?" Shitty looked at Fat Dobey knowing he had some more information.

"Well, it's an old head nigga name Fats around y'all joint. Dat fucks wit' one of my old heads and he paid a nigga ten bands to get up on you. You know who dat nigga is?" Fat Dobey said with a funny look on his face.

"Yeah, I know who dat is. Dat nigga scared as shit! But who da nigga dat came through hittin'?" Shitty got upset thinking about how Fats put some money on his head.

"Look, I fuck wit' da nigga. It's one of my mans. But money talks, I'm fucked up. Give me ten bands and I'll tell you da nigga's name and throw up the alley," Fat Dobey said being the snake he is for a bag.

"Bet," Shitty said going in his pocket to see how much money he had on him. "Damn all I got is forty-seven hundred on me right now," Shitty said with his money in his hands. "But I'll give you four bands right now and the other six band after you hold up your end."

"Bet," Fat Dobey said thirsty. "When you gonna be ready? I'll have him ready for you tonight."

"Nah, sumthin' tomorrow though for sure." Shitty handed Fat Dobey $4000 of his money and put the rest in his pocket.

"A'ight dat's a bet," Fat Dobey said excited putting the four bands in his pockets. But the dude around my way name Lil Snook."

"Bet say less," Shitty said, giving Fat Dobey dap as they walked back toward Shy and Turk.

"A'ight I'm gone, bra. Hit me asap. Salaam Alaykum," Fat Dobey said, walking off.

Shy and Turk got in Shitty's, car ready to go back around their hood. As soon as all them were in the car Shitty looked at Shy and Turk and said, "Man shit 'bout to get real around da Yo for real." Shitty started his 300c and pulled off going back around his hood.

After dropping Shy and Turk off back down Ridge Road Shitty pulled up down Stoneridge and parked. He rolled up a blunt of O.G. and called Squirt.

Squirt answered on the third ring. "YoYo?"

"What it do, bra? Where da fuck you at?" Shitty asked lighting up his blunt of O.G. takin' a hit.

"I'm over Shantel's joint fuckin' wit' lil' Malik. Why, what's up?"

"Man, I just found out who came through hittin' and hit Baby Boy." Shitty was getting amped up.

"Oh, yeah. Who the fuck was it? And where da fuck you find dat out at?" Squirt was geekin' to see who their next vick was about to be.

"Man, I don't know da lil dude, but his name is Lil' Snook, he from down the Farms. You heard of slim before?" Shitty said, choking on the blunt of O.G.

"Fuck yeah. Dat's my man Lil Gary from down the Farms man. I don't know him, but my man used to talk about him when we was locked up. But I'm 'bout to hit him and see what's up wit' shorty," Squirt said ready to hang up wit' Shitty and call his man Lil' Gary.

"Nah, fuck all dat. I got a good man dat's going to throw me an alley tomorrow night. I'ma slam dunk it. Ain't no need to call slim 'bout nothin'." Shitty yelled at Squirt getting mad that he'd even think about calling a nigga that wasn't in their circle that is close with their vick, which could put him on point and back fire on them.

"Fuck dat shit then. Say less, but I don't get it. Why the fuck shorty come through hittin'? Ain't nobody ever get into it wit' them." Squirt was confused about why somebody they wasn't beefin' with or had no problem with would shoot their block up.

"Kill, dat's a fact! But money talks and my alias said Fats big scared ass put ten bands on me and your head," Shitty said, laughing like money being on they heads was a joke.

"What?" Squirt yelled shocked of what he was hearing.

"Yeah, slim! See big boy did dat on some snake shit, for us robbing Zo. "See he felt if he got me or you out of the picture first, it would be easier to get at everybody else, or whatever he was thinking," Shitty said dead serious.

"Yeah, I'm thinking 'bout dat shit now. He most definitely was thinking sumthin' on them terms. So, what's up? What we gonna do?" Squirt said ready to get at Fats.

"Nah, we gonna act like we don't know he tried to bring us a move. And when dat time is right, we're gonna get all over him," Shitty said. "But we're gonna get all over da lil dude Snook tomorrow night."

"Bet, say less. Hit me whenever you ready," Squirt said.

"You already know. I'ma hit you later on. I'm 'bout to go fuck wit' dis lil bitch down the West right quick. Love for Life," Shitty said.

"A'ight bet. Love for Life," Squirt replied back as dey both ended their call as.

Shitty pulled off from down Stoneridge heading down Southwest.

CHAPTER 12

"YoYo," Flip said, walking up on Shitty and Mari with Keda smoking on some purple haze he'd just brought from up top.

"YoYo," They replied.

Shitty and Mari were behind Shitty's grandmother's house just chilling and making small talk waiting for Turk and Baby Boy to pull back up with the liquor they drove to go get. Mari was a young nigga from down bottom dat Shitty took under his wing after he took a gun charge for him when the police jumped out down bottom and found Shitty coat with a gun in it on the gate. Mari stepped up when the police was about to lock Shitty up without being asked, too. Knowing that Shitty had just come home two months before and was sure to be gone for at least another five years if booked for a gun.

Mari did fifteen months in jail. Mari was 5'8, one-hundred and fifty-five pounds, light-brown-skinned with a beard, and a low haircut with waves.

When Shitty looked up and saw Keda wit' Flip he started joking with her like he always did not knowing that a couple of weeks ago his lil' brother Loc and KGR robbed her.

"Damn, fat girl where da fuck you been in the house hiding? You act like a nigga trying rob you or sumthin'. You ain't da only motherfucker gettin' no money," Shitty joked with Keda pulling a knot of money out his pocket.

"Nah, I been around for real. But I been supposed to hit your phone and holla at you about sumthin'." Keda smiled.

"What's up, you good? What you need to hold sumthin'?" Shitty said serious because he and Keda went way back and always borrowed money from each other.

"I do for real, but dat's not what I wanted to holla at you 'bout. You know your lil' brova and Lil' Chris robbed me like two weeks ago," Keda said, calling KGR by his real name shaking her head.

"What?" Shitty said, shocked.

"Yeah, slim, dey took like ten bands off me, slapped me wit' da dog and everything," Keda said looking at Shitty who was getting mad by the second.

"Where the fuck KGR and Loc lil' asses?" Shitty yelled to Mari.

"I don't know. I ain't seen dem niggas since earlier. You already know dey was in. But I'm 'bout to try to hit both of dey phone," Mari said, pulling out his iPhone 10 to call Loc and KGR.

"Moe, I'ma fuck Loc's lil' bitch ass up. Here go five bands right here. I'll give you five bands later. I'ma get it from Squirt when he comes out cause I ain't got it on me. And Loc and KGR split dat shit and dat's his lil' brova," Shitty said giving Keda the five bands he brought outside, which was all he had on him.

"Nah, dis' good right here, bra. Don't worry 'bout dat other shit. I appreciate you," Keda said, putting the five bands in her pocket and giving him a hug.

"Dem niggas phone going to voicemail," Mari said to Shitty shaking his head.

85

"Fuck dem, I'ma catch dey lil' asses. What makes it so funny is that dem lil' niggas been around me like twenty times and ain't never say shit," Shitty said laughing.

"Nah, what's funny is dey robbed me at like two-thirty in the morning. I was in the house sleeping. My mother woke me up talking 'bout Lil Malik came to the door looking for me and said it's a big dice game down bottom and dat you sent him to get me cause dey was sweet," Keda said thinking back on how them youngins tricked her.

"Kill!" Flip yelled as him, Mari and Keda kept laughing.

Shitty ain't laugh, he ain't see nothing funny about Loc and KGR using his name to rob Keda cause if it would've been somebody else it could've easily gotten him killed. What made him even madder was that they ain't never tell him about it and it had been weeks.

"Y'all laughin', but I'ma fuck Loc up for real," Shitty warned as Flip handed him the blunt of Purple Haze he was smoking.

"YoYo! Y'all lackin'. I could've smoke all y'all asses," Day-Day said, sneaking up on them from behind.

"What it do, brah? Where the fuck you just come from? A nigga ain't even see your lil' ass," Flip said dapping up Day-Day.

"I just came out of Janay's joint. Y'all right here laughing hard as shit, I heard y'all in there," Day-Day said talking about a girl he be slightly fucking with that lives next door to Shitty's grandmother's house.

"What the fuck wit' you, nigga? You lookin' all mad and shit," Day-Day said to Shitty.

"Nah, I'm coolin', bra. But those wild niggas Loc and KGR bagged Keda for ten bands." Shitty looked at Keda as he started busting out laughing.

"Dem young niggas be lunchin', kill," Day-Day laughing hard is shit.

"Nah, for real, but fuck dat shit. I gotta holla at you right quick," Shitty said to Day-Day as him and Day-Day walked to the side of his grandmother house leaving Flip, Keda and Mari out of listening range. Once they got to the side of the house Shitty got straight to the point. "Ay, brah, I found out who hit Baby Boy," Shitty said, looking at Day-Day, smiling.

"Why da fuck you smiling? Who was it and where da fuck dey at?" Day-Day was geeking to kill whoever shot his brother.

"Some lil' dude named, Snook from da Farms," Shitty said. "But look, I got a play for him tonight. A nigga he be with thirsty and gonna back door him for us."

"Oh, yeah, say less. But why da fuck da nigga Snook came through hittin'? We beefin' or ever got into it with the Farm?" Day-Day was not understanding why a nigga they had no issues with would just come through their block trying to kill somebody.

"Mannn, it's a long story. I'ma tell you in a minute. Plus, I got to find Loc and KGR lil asses," Shitty said not feeling like telling Day-Day the whole story about Fat's unforgivable betrayal.

"A'ight, but Loc and KGR just went in Lil' Choo-Choo's house with him and Drock 'bout twenty minutes ago. Dey might still be in dere," Day-Day said to Shitty.

"Bet, I'm 'bout to walk over Lil' Choo-Choo's house and fuck Loc and KGR up. I'ma hit your phone in a couple of hours so we can slide down da Farms and get over dat situation," Shitty said to Day-Day dapping him up as he headed to Lil' Choo-Choo's house.

Day-Day walked back around the back of Shitty's grandmother's house with Flip, Keda and Mari.

"Loc, you got skunked pass da joystick. Dats twenty-one to nothin'," Lil Choo-Choo said.

"Man, I get a chance, I got the ball if I don't score dat's game," Loc said not trying to give up the controller.

Loc, Lil Choo-Choo, KGR and Drock was in Lil' Choo-Choo's house playing Madden 2020 on Playstation 4, and Drock had Loc 21-0 in the first quarter of the game. Drock and Lil' Choo-Choo were young niggas who grew up with Loc and KGR and was just like them. They're all bullshit and be geeked to rob or shoot anybody for the slightest reason. Drock and Lil' Choo-Choo was both light-brown-skinned. Lil' Choo-Choo was probably a bit lighter and both stood 5'6. Drock had a shortcut, and Lil' Choo-Choo had short dreadlocks. Drock was also about one-hundred and seventy pounds, while Lil' Choo-Choo about one-hundred and fifty pounds. They were just like Loc and KGR, you rarely saw one without the other.

"Moe, dat's it!" KGR yelled as Loc just went for the first down on the game and got stopped.

"Damn you geeking like shit to play," Loc said, throwing KGR the PS4 controller.

As Loc threw KGR the controller they heard somebody knocking on the front door. Being that it was Lil' Choo-Choo's house he went to answer it. Lil' Choo-Choo opened the door without asking who it was like most people in the hood do.

"What's up, Lil' Choo? Where Loc and KGR at?" Shitty asked soon as Lil' Choo-Choo opened the door.

"Oh, what's up, big bra? Dey upstairs, come on in," Lil' Choo-Choo said, letting Shitty all the way inside.

As soon as Shitty got upstairs in Lil' Choo-Choo's room where Loc, Drock and KGR were at playing the game, the three of them saw him and immediately knew something was up. Because Shitty had never been in Lil' Choo-Choo's and rarely ever be around the young niggas.

"What's up, bra?" Loc asked soon as he locked eyes with his brother knowing Shitty was in Lil' Choo-Choo's house for a reason.

"You know what's up. Why the fuck y'all rob Keda?" Shitty yelled as he walked up to Loc and punched him five straight times in his chest and arms, before turning to KGR and hitting him with a three-piece.

"Hold Moe," KGR said caught off guard by Shitty punching him and covering up on the bed.

Lil' Choo-Choo and Drock just looked in silence shocked because they ain't even know KGR and Loc robbed tomboy Keda.

"And y'all niggas better bring me the five bands later that I gave dat bitch back," Shitty said, getting mad still looking at KGR and Loc who had dumb looks on their faces.

"Man, we ain't got no five bands. We ain't tell you to give dat bitch shit back," Loc said to his brother in a little over a mumble mad dat he just beat him up.

"Nigga you still talkin'? Loc don't make me fuck you up in here. Y'all better go find a move cause I want my five bands today," Shitty barked, looking back and forth from Loc and KGR. "And y'all gonna use my name to get her outside. I should really fuck y'all up. Y'all know dat coulda got a nigga killed? Y'all niggas need to start thinkin' for real!" Shitty fumed shaking his head. "But I'ma let y'all sucka asses get a pass. Y'all better have my money before the day's out, or I'ma fuck y'all up every day until I get my shit." Shitty stormed out of the room, down the stairs and out the front door leaving

Loc, KGR, Drock and Lil' Choo-Choo still in the room shock and half scared.

About a whole two minutes went by before KGR broke the silence. "Bra we got to find a move like asap so we can give Shitty his five bands back. He ain't 'bout to be keep hittin' on me. I told your dumb ass don't use his name!" KGR yelled at Loc.

"Shut your scared ass up. We gonna get him his money," Loc said as they all went back to normal playing the PS4

⬤ ⬤ ⬤ ⬤ ⬤ ⬤

11:00 dat night Shitty, Day-Day and Mari was in a stolen dark blue 2019 Dodge Charger with tinted windows heading down Barry Farms. Shitty had just gotten off the phone with Fat Dobey. Fat Dobey said he set the play up for them to get at Lil' Snook who came through their block a week ago and shot at Squirt and almost killed Day-Day's brother Baby Boy.

Fat Dobey told Snook he had two men out of VA. 'bout to come through and buy some weed, and for him to wait since they were the only two outside, knowing Lil' Snook wasn't going leave him outside by himself so late at night.

As soon as Shitty pulled up on Summers Road in Barry Farms he saw Fat Dobey and the dude Lil' Snook. They were smoking and talking shit on somebody's front porch. Shitty parked the Charger and Day-Day and Mari got out with one thing on their mind, Murder!

"Damn, what's up, nigga?" Fat Dobey yelled to Mari as him and Day-Day approached him and Lil Snook.

"Shit! What's up, fat boy?" Mari replied, giving Fat Doby dap.

"What's up with dat weed? I got fifty," Mari said, getting straight to business, ducking the small talk.

"I got him," Lil Snook said to Fat Dobey pulling out three dub bags of weed.

"Nah, I got him. I only got three dubs left. My other man 'bout to pull up for one-hunnid dollars, you can get dat," Fat Dobey said playing it off like a pro knowing he ain't have nobody else coming and if he did Lil' Snook would be dead before they got there.

"Bet, say no more," Lil Snook said geekin to catch the $100 sell.

"Come on, my shit in da back," Fat Dobey said to Mari walking off heading to the back of the alley with Mari on his heels.

As soon as Day-Day ain't see Mari and Fat Dobey he whipped out his black Glock 27.

"Hold, Slim, you good round here?" Lil Snook said as Day-Day whipped out his Glock.

"Yeah, I'm already sharp. You ain't tho'" Day-Day said as he pointed his Glock at Lil' Snook's head and fired three shots.

Bop! Bop! Bop!

Lil Snook hit the ground with a loud thump and Day-Day hit him five more times just to make sure he was dead.

Bop! Bop! Bop! Bop! Bop!

"Dat's for my brova bitch ass nigga!" Day-Day yelled as he jogged off to the car.

Mari and Fat Dobey were not even all the way in the back of the alley before they heard the sound of the first shots being fired, but soon as they did Mari whipped out his P.89 Ruger and turned it on Fat Dobey.

"Hold, Slim, Shitty like my..." Fat Dobey was saying before Mari filled him up with six bullets in the face and chest as he crumbled up on the ground lifeless.

91

"Dis what happens when you snake your man, goofy ass nigga!" Mari yelled as he ran back to the car.

Mari and Day-Day rushed back to the car, as Day-Day was opening the passenger door Mari was right behind him 'bout to open the back door. Once they were both in the Charger, Shitty pulled off smooth as possible to draw no attention to their car.

"So, y'all good?" Shitty asked, looking at Day-Day and Mari once he had stop at the red light by Anacostia Subway Station.

"You already know," Day-Day said to Shitty why Mari just smiled.

"Say less," Shitty said and pulled off as the light turned green heading back around the Yo.

CHAPTER 13

The next morning Shitty was at his grandmother's house with Mello, Fat Marcus, and his little cousin Jose, playing *'Call of Duty'* on XBOX ONE. Shitty had come up to his grandmother's house about two hours ago after dropping his girl Mook off to work so he could holler at Mello, who slept over the night before after the club.

"On God, dey was rocking like shit last night!" Mello said to Fat Marcus, who ain't go out to the club because he had to work.

"Yea, I heard," Fat Marcus replied, looking at Mello shaking his head mad he missed out on another night of action.

"Yea, slim we looked sweet in dere on dem people last night," Shitty said joining in on the conversation after pausing the game and putting down the joystick.

"Rico, let me play now. You got killed like 3 times!" cried his little 12 year old cousin Jose, calling him by his real name.

"Aite, I'ma let you play in a minute, but go in grandma's room right quick and let me holla at Mello about sumtin," said Shitty.

Jose who got up off the bed without responding and left the room, heading to his grandmother's room. After Jose was gone, Shitty turned his attention back to Mello and Fat Marcus.

"Yea, I was about to say cuz, what the fuck is up on that play with Guala scared ass? You playing, but dat nigga ain't to be trusted. It's just a matter of time before he snakes you out. Shame ain't got no morals. You got to remember dat slim!" Shitty said to Mello trying to get him to take Guala snake ways serious before it was too late.

"I'm already hip cuz. I'm on it. I'm just trying to figure out how to backdoor him without it coming back to haunt me. I'm tryna hit him, but im not tryna get bagged for it," Mello said dead serious.

"Man, I feel you cuz, but you got to figure out something fast or if you want, I'll let my man Lil Sike from Trinidad come around here and get up on him," Shitty said trying to give Mello a way out from getting his hands dirty.

"Dats cool, but I don't want no nigga dat ain't from around here to come around here and do nothing. Dat shit just don't sit right with me. But don't worry about it cuz. Before next week I'ma put something together," Mello said in deep thought.

"Man, I'm about to go in the house and wash my ass. What y'all bout to do?" Fatmarcus asked, breaking his long silence and trying to switch the mode up.

"I ain't bout to do shit, for real. I got to go meet June and Bow later on. They tryna holla at me about some shit. So I'ma cool out until den," Shitty said to Fat Marcus as he grabbed the joystick up getting ready to finish playing Call of Duty.

Mello was still in deep thought with his head down trying to come up with a plan to kill Guala when Fatmarcus broke his thoughts.

"What you bout to do, bra? You all in the zone and shit!" Fat Marcus said to Mello snapping him out of his daze.

"I'm bout to go down bottom in YaYa house and fuck with C Roc," Mello said getting up off the bed. He grabbed his Armani Exchange sweater and put it on. As Mello was getting himself together, Shitty unpaused the Call of Duty game and started back playing. Soon as Shitty unpaused the game you would've thought his little cousin Jose had a silent alarm on it the way he ran back into the room.

"Rico, y'all finish now! Now can I play?" Jose asked.

"Damn, Moe. You was in the hallway dat whole time waiting, neckin'? We just got finished. You geekin' like shit, huh!" Shitty said to his little cousin Jose, passing him the joystick. Jose just smiled.

"Man, we gone, cuz! I'ma hit your phone later on," said Mello.

"Aite, that's a bet!" Shitty replied as he dapped Mello and Fat Marcus up as they headed out the room to leave. Once they were gone, Shitty turned his focus back to his little cousin Jose who was deep in his zone playing the game.

"CJ what time your mother gets off work?" Shitty asked Jose, calling him by his nickname.

"I don't know! She don't ever come straight home from work," Jose said without taking his attention off the game.

"Aite, hide dis gun for me. I'll be back in a little bit," Shitty said, taking his Glock 26 with a 30 off his waist and handing it to Jose like he'd done hundreds of times. After Shitty gave Jose the gun, he left the room and went out the back door and headed to his car. He was ready to ride out to MD to meet his old head June and Bow.

30 minutes later...

Shitty was inside his old head house with Bow. Just two days ago Shitty had robbed an older dude named 'Ro' that was from down the bottom of the Yo that June gambled and fucked with. Ro liked to fuck with younger girls and tried to fuck with the wrong one, Shitty's sister Dime.

Dime told Shitty for three months straight that every time Ro sees her he would try to talk to her and harass her. Shitty told Ro at least three times too many not to say anything to his little sister and to leave her alone. He only shot him warnings out of the respect he had for June. But Ro was a 47 year old creep that loved to fuck with young girls. It didn't matter how old she was, if she looked old enough, he would fuck her. His downfall came being that Shitty's sister Dime was nothing but 17.

Shitty caught Ro at one in the morning in front of his brother Big South house around a hood called Lincoln Heights, getting in his two door red Corvette. He robbed and pistol whipped him until he was damn near dead. After Shitty finally finished beating Ro with his gun, he gave him one last warning that if he say anything else to his little sister, he was going to kill him the next time he sees him.

Now two days later his old head June wanted to holler at him out of the blue. So Shitty already knew what he wanted or was going to talk to him about. When he arrived June and Bow was sitting in June's dining room drinking Preach C'iroc talking about just that.

"Yea, tho Shitty, you gotta chill out! You know Ro's been a creep, slim. I see where you coming from because dat's little sis, but at least give slim a pass for me and give dat money back," June pleaded to Shitty who was now sipping on his cup of Ciroc looking at June like he was crazy.

June is dark skinned and reminded you of the actor Tyrese off the movie 'Babyboy'. He was real and solid as they come, and was funny as shit, but when it was time to get serious, he stopped all the joking fast. June had watched Shitty and the rest of his crew grow up since they were in elementary school. Due to Shitty being the worst youngin around the Yo since he was knee high, and the first one to jump off the porch with the older boys, June took to him the most.

Shitty was like a little brother to June. Any time Shitty and his crew get into it with the old heads, June was the one who would always come and holler at them because he was the ONLY one they fucked with enough to listen to. Anyone else could meet their glizzy and they knew that.

"I hear you big boy, but you knew me since I was a young nigga. I'm not giving no money back. Dat shit dead! I told slim creep ass like five times not to say shit to her and he Ray Charles a nigga like I was a wild nigga. Da only reason I ain't kill him was because of you," Shitty said to June, dead serious. Anyone that knew Shitty, or anyone in his crew, knew that if they robbed or took something from someone, that it was a lock. They wasn't giving nothing back.

"Shidddd fuck dat shit den shorty. I tried! I told dat nigga a thousand times somebody was going to fuck around and kill his ass for fucking with their young daughter or sister," June said shaking his head.

"Damn, Bow. You quiet as shit! What sup bra?" Shitty said to Bow who was right there listening to them smiling.

Bow was three years older than Shitty and the only young nigga that jumped off the porch as young as him. Due to him being three years older, he was the only one that's been in the streets before him. Shitty had much love and respect for Bow and vice versa.

"I'm coolin', little bra. I was just imagining how scared that nigga Ro was when you was robbing him. I know he thought you was gonna burn his creep ass up!" Bow said and they all started laughing.

"Nah, for real. You would've thought I was that nigga's mother beating his ass with a belt the way he kept screaming. I swear I ain't gonna do it again!" Shitty said, pretending to be Ro as they all continued laughing hard as shit. Shitty, June and Bow continued to drink, talk shit and laugh, for another hour or so before Shitty finally got up ready to leave.

"Look, I'm gone, slim. I'ma see y'all niggas later on or sumtin'. I gotta go check my traps." Shitty said as he got up from the table.

"Aite, make sure you hit my phone later young nigga," June said as he got up and dapped Shitty up and gave him a hug.

"Say less!" Shitty replied back as he broke June embrace and dapped Bow up and headed out the door. He got in his car and headed back around Yo to see what he could get into today.

* * * * * *

"Ay, wat da fuck dat blister sellin?" Lil E asked Nine. Lil E, Nine, and Lil Choo Choo, was down at the Double R chillin'. They had been down there for about three hours hustling with Turk and Babyboy. Turk and Babyboy had just rode off to KFC to get something to eat, and soon as they pulled off, a gay man walked up trying to sell some stolen designer belts and shirts. He had one bag full of Gucci, LV, Versace, and Balmain shirts. In another bag he had belts to match.

"He got some designer belts and shirts an shit. Dat's where Turk be getting all dem belts an shit from," Lil Choo Choo said to Lil E, speaking up for Nine who had no idea what the man was selling.

"Oh, yea? Y'all tryna bag him!?" Lil E said, smiling at Nine and Lil Choo Choo.

"You know I don't care! Choo, call his gay ass over here," Nine said, smiling and geeking to put some work in.

"Aite." Lil Choo Choo said, laughing as he called the gay man over to them. When the man heard Lil Choo Choo calling him, he came without a second thought. He knew that every time he came around Double R he always sells out of all his stuff.

"Hey y'all? Y'all tryna get some of dis shit?" The man said in a gay sounding voice.

"Yea, what you got today?" Lil E said, reaching for the bags trying to look inside.

"Hold up little boy! Don't touch nothing until you put some coins in my hand." The gay man yelled at Lil E as he snatched his bags away from him and put his hand out so he could put some money in it.

"Damn, you holding your hand out and shit. You ain't even tell us what you got or how much it cost!" Lil Choo Choo said as he whipped out a knot of money and flashing it in the gay man's face. Soon as the man saw Lil Choo Choo with a knot of money he started to look in his bags to see exactly what he had to offer. When Lil E saw him looking through his bags, not paying them any attention, he gives Nine, who was the closest to him, the signal. Nine whipped out his P.89 Ruger with a 30 and grabbed the gay man by his shirt and put his gun in his face.

"Bitch, you know wat the fuck time it is. If you buck or scream on some faggy shit I'ma smoke your ass, by Allah!" Nine yelled, dead serious. He wished the man called his bluff so he could kill him.

"I'm not goin' to buck little boy. Please don't shoot me! Y'all can have dis shit. A bitch can steal some more," The man said scared to death, dropping his bags.

Lil E grabbed both bags why Lil Choo Choo went in the man's pockets, taking everything but his keys. After Nine sees that Lil Choo Choo was finished going through his pockets, and Lil E already had the bags, he pushed the man and kicked him in his ass. "Get the fuck outta here!"

As the man got in his car and drove off, they jogged off heading to Lil Choo Choo's to see what they came off with.

CHAPTER 14

It was five o'clock in the afternoon and Shitty was around 22nd on the other side of southeast with KGR. He had just gotten off the phone with a good man by the name of J Roc. He promised him to ride around his neighborhood and drop off $250 to a friend of his name Zo for him.

Shitty had met J Roc when he was locked up in the pen in Pollock, Louisiana. J Roc was still in the pen doing 40 years and every time he called Shitty he made sure he handled whatever J Roc needed done. There wasn't too many niggas like Shitty still running around. Most niggas give away a lot of false promises to good solid men that they were doing time with when they was behind the wall. Not Shitty. Everything he promised the men he was behind the wall with, Shitty did it, and more. If you needed money, pictures, an affidavit signed, a bitch, or even a nigga, he got it done. If you needed a rat taken care of Shitty was all over it. If he fucked with you, there was no questions asked.

Shitty parked and got out his car with KGR on his heels. The dude Zo that Shitty come to meet for J Roc, was a light skinned dude about 6'6" and rocked long dreadlocks that hung to his waist. Shitty had been locked up with Zo before as well, so when J Roc mentioned meeting him, he already knew who he was going to meet. When Shitty got out the car, he saw Zo and another dark skinned dude by the name of Squirrel, standing in front of a building smoking.

"Wat it do, big boy?" Shitty said to Zo giving him some dap as he and KGR walked up.

"Shit, how you bro?" Zo replied back with a smile.

"I'm not on shit, coolin'. Huh, J Roc told me to put dis cash in your hand," Shitty said, passing Zo the $250 that he counted out for J Roc.

"Aite, dat's a bet. I just got off da phone with slim too. He told me you was about to pull up," Zo said taking the money form Shitty and putting it in his pockets.

"Damn Squirrel, what's sup?" Shitty said to Squirrel who was in a light daze.

"My bad slim. I'm not on shit coolin'. I'm high as shit" Squirrel said, his eyes barely open as he looked at Shitty clearly high out his mind.

"Yea, I see!" Shitty said, and they all bust out laughing.

"Ay y'all dirty!? That's them people right dere," Zo said to Shitty and KGR as he spotted a dark blue old Ford Taurus sedan with tinted windows slowly driving by. Those were the police that was known as 'jumpouts'.

"Yea, slim. Y'all might as well roll out, because dem people about to buck a U, unless y'all tryna come in da trap and chill?" Zo asked, taking the bags of crack he had in his pockets and putting them in his ass.

"Nah, we good. We got shit to do. I'ma hit your phone sometime next week big boy!" Shitty said as he and KGR dapped Zo and Squirrel up before jogging back to his car while they headed for the trap. Once back in the car. Shitty started it up as quick as possible and pulled off in a hurry. He wasn't trying to be nowhere in sight when the police rode back through.

Later that night Shitty and his crew were on another move. Shitty got a call from his man Bow 30 minutes ago that yesterday, after he left from talking with him and June, Ro came over with his brother Big South. He said that they were trying to get revenge for what he did to Ro either by Big South killing him, or one of his little brother's, when a good time presented itself.

So Shitty, Flip, Squirt and Day-Day , was now back around Lincold Heights, where Big South lived with his wife. Bow gave Shitty the scoop on what time Big South comes home from work and what time he should be in. Shitty and his crew had only been in front of Big Souths' house for about 15 minutes before he finally pulled up

It was 11:25 pm and Bow said that Big South had gotten off work at 11:00 pm, but should be home no later than 11:30pm, and he was 100% right. Flip was in the driver seat of a stolen white Dodge Caravan while Shitty was in the passenger seat. Squirt and Dayday sat in the back. They all wore face masks and was ready to put in some work.

When Big South pulled up in the circle of Lincoln Heights he parked his car. Shitty, Squirt and Day-Day was out the car with the quickness and up on Big South's gold Silverado pick-up truck before he could even get all the way out the car. Once they got up on him, Squirt opened the door that was already unlocked. Shitty grabbed Big South by his neck and put his Mac 10 in his face.

"What's going on?" Big South said in a frightened voice, scared to death at seeing three gunmen all over him, and pulling him out his truck.

"Shut da fuck up and walk. Try anything crazy and you gonna hear how a Mac sounds," Shitty said as he, Squirt, and Day-Day walked Big South to his front door.

"Wat da fuck you waiting for! Open da muther fuckin' door!" Day-Day yelled from behind him and smacked him with his Glock 27 with a 30, in the back of his head.

"Ughhhhh. Fuck, slim. I'ma open da door, chill out!" Big South cried out as he pulled out his keys and opened his front door. Once inside, Day-Day closed the door behind them as they made Big South get on his knees with his hands locked behind his head.

"Baby, you home already?" a woman's voice said coming from the kitchen area of the house.

As soon as he heard a woman's voice Shitty reacted. He turned to Day-Day . "Go make sure nobody's upstairs." He then turned to Squirt. "Go grab his wife and bring her in the living room."

Big South had a three bedroom house that was fairly small, so it ain't take no time for Dayday to make sure no one else was home. As he was coming back down the stairs to let Shitty know that it wasn't nobody else home, they heard what sounded like scuffling coming from the kitchen.

Shitty kept his gun pointed at Big South's head as Dayday went to see what the fuck was going on with Squirt, but Shitty already had an idea. Day-Day walked into the kitchen with his Glock 27 in his hand, ready to shoot anything in sight. When he got in the kitchen, all he saw was a light skinned woman with a short haircut on the ground with a bloody face, and she looked dead. Squirt had his hand on his side, gun still in hand, bending over, breathing hard. It was clear to see he was out of breath.

"Damn, bra. Wat the fuck happened!?" Day-Day yelled to Squirt, still slightly in shock form what he was looking at.

"What it look like! I had to knock dat bitch out. Dat bitch started fightin' me. She scratched me in my face and everything," Squirt yelled to Day-Day shaking his head. He was still trying to catch his breath.

"Bra you got to cut dat bitch hands off. You know dem people will..." Day-Day stopped what he was saying when he heard four shots from Shitty's Mac go off in the front room.

Blatt! Blatt! Blatt! Blatt!

Shitty fired his Mac 10 in the back of Big South's head and his brains and blood spattered everywhere. He fell face first on his living room floor. "Y'all ready?" Shitty called out to Squirt and Day-Day as they came running in the room.

"Yea!" Squirt replied, answering for him and Day-Day . He was ready to get the fuck out of the house after Shitty fired shots from his Mac 10. That shit was loud as fuck and he knew more than likely that Big South's neighbors had heard the shots.

"Hold up Moe! You got to kill dat bitch and cut her hands off. She got your DNA under her nails. Dem people going to link you to dat shit," Day-Day yelled to Squirt giving him law. He knew that if he ain't kill and cut the woman's hands off, he was surely going to go to jail within the next couple of weeks and for a very long time.

"Man, you lunchin' Q! I'ma kill da bitch, but I'm not cutting her hands off. Dats on some other shit," Squirt yelled to Day-Day , looking at him like he was crazy.

"Aite, you playin'. Fuck it den. You gonna be the one over the wall," Day-Day said, shaking his head, looking at Squirt like he was dumb. Squirt jogged back in the kitchen and shot Big South wife three times point blank range in her face with his Glock 30 and came back in the front room like nothing happened.

"Y'all ready now?" Squirt asked, looking at Shitty and Day-Day , ready to get the fuck out of Big South's house.

105

"Yea, we gone!" Shitty said as they all headed out the front door. As they were opening the front door Flip was about to come inside.

"Holdddd up, Moe!" Shitty yelled, shocked at being caught off guard. He pointed his Mac 10 at Flip's face and Flip pointed his Beretta 9 at his as well. Flip felt that something must have gone wrong in Big South's house due to them taking so long. They were only suppose to kill Big South and come right back, which they could've done without going in the house.

"Come on, Moe! You taking all mutherfuckin day. I thought he killed y'all in dere," Flip yelled as he withdrew his gun and ran back to their stolen Caravan, with his crew right behind him. Once back inside the Caravan, Flip pulled off and headed back around the Yo.

● ● ● ● ● ●

10 minutes later....

Flip pulled up around the Yo to the alley.

"Y'all go head and get out! I'ma go park dis over on Ely," Flip said as he stopped in front of their trap and let them out. Once everyone hopped out, he pulled back off to get rid of the stolen caravan. When Shitty, Squirt and Day-Day got out the caravan, Day-Day was on Squirt's line about not cutting Big South's wife hands off.

"Moe, why you ain't cut dat bitch hands off?" Day-Day asked Squirt, still clearly upset and thinking about the evidence that the police are going to have on them. Well, at least Squirt.

"Slim, you still talkin' about dat shit! I'm not cutting nobody muther fuckin' hands off. Why da fuck you ain't do it

106

if you so noid?!" Squrit yelled, mad that Day-Day still was bringing up cutting somebody's hands off.

"Nigga, you da one noid as shit! You scared to cut a bitch hands off to stop from going to jail for life. Why would I cut da bitch hands off? She ain't scratch me!" Day-Day yelled to Squirt, now really in his feelings since Squirt called him noid, when he was just worried about freedom.

"Aite, bra. I'm not bout to argue with you. Dat shit over with now," Squirt said, sensing Day-Day getting mad and didn't want to keep arguing. Especially when he knew Day-Day was 100% right. He just wasn't with cutting nobody's hands off or any body part for that matter.

Shitty was just letting them go back and forth because he felt both of their points and didn't want to take sides. He just waited until they stopped arguing by themselves.

"Look, what you niggas about to do?" Shitty asked Squirt and Day-Day once they was finished arguing.

"I'm about to go in the house and change my clothes and fix something to eat right quick,"Squirt said to Shitty, rubbing his stomach. "What the fuck you bout to do?" Squirt continued.

"I'm about to ride out to Baltimore to holla at a good man I fuck with right quick," said Shitty. Day-Day wasn't paying either one of them no mind. He was still mad at Squirt because he knew it was a matter of time before the police would be knocking his door down.

"Day-Day , wat you bout to do, bra?" Shitty asked, getting his attention back.

"I don't know. I guess I'ma chill out here and try to sell some of dat coke I just bought earlier from Turk," he said sounding nonchalant.

"Shit. Aite, I'm gone! I'ma see y'all later on. If something comes up, hit my phone," Shitty said to Squrit and Day-Day as he dapped them both up, and headed down Stoneride to get in his car to head out to Baltimore.

"Look, I'm gone too, bra. Ill be back out later on," Squirt said to Day-Day .

"Aite!" Day-Day said as he dapped Squirt up.

He headed to the trap while Squirt walked in the opposite direction heading to his Camaro that was parked in the alley.

CHAPTER 15

"Moe, do y'all ever leave the trap or go get some pussy?"Mac asked as he walked in YaYa apartment and closed the door behind him. Squirt, Turk, Mac and Mello, was Down Bottom in YaYa house, trapping it out as always. They had been sitting in there for the last couple of hours just smoking, and waiting for crack and weed sells ,and bullshitting around.

"Nigga, do your mutherfuckin' head ever stop growin'? You gigantic M&M head bitch!" Turk replied to Mac, joking as always as everybody busted out laughing.

"Nah, for real. Y'all be in dis joint all day," Mac said as he stopped laughing.

"We tryna get to a bag, cuz," said Turk.

"Yea, but I can't sit in dis dirty ass joint all day," said Mac, dead serious as he looked around the apartment. YaYa's apartment was a real trap house. It was trash, weed bags, dirty clothes, and used condoms. You name it, and it was everywhere in her apartment.

"Yea, I feel you, but dis dirty ass joint do numbers," Mello said as he passed the dro to Turk.

"Yea, I'm hip! I just came down here to holla at y'all. Well, Squirt anyway," Mac said, looking at Squirt.

"Mac, what's sup big boy?" Squirt said, looking at Mac with a smile on his face.

"Cuz, what's sup wit y'all youngins and Fats, sir? Dat nigga don't even be wanting to come in da alley anymore. Dat nigga think y'all goin' do sumtin' to him or sumtin'," Mac said to Squirt with a worried look on his face.

"Man, fuck dat nigga cuz. Dat nigga a snake! He tried some shit and dat's all I'ma say. But we ain't thinking bout dat nigga," Squirt said to Mac, keeping him in the blind about the snake shit Fats did and about what they really had planned for him. Squirt knew if he said anything sideways to Mac about Fats, he would go back and run his mouth and fuck up their whole plan that they had yet to put together.

"Yea, cuz, I know y'all ain't worried about dat nigga. I keep tellin' him dat, but he on some noid shit. But don't worry about it. I'ma holla at him later on and let him know I hollered at you and dat all's well," Mac said to Squirt, glad that he reassured him that Shitty and his crew wasn't trying to harm Fats.

"Say less, cuz!" Squirt said to Mac smiling. He dapped Mac up and he turned around and left out of YaYa' apartment with a false sense of relief.

"Let me hit dat!" Squirt yelled to Turk as he passed him the blunt of dro. As Squirt inhaled the dro smoke, all he could do was laugh to himself thinking about how scared Mac just sounded for Fats. Yet, at the same time, he knew that he had the right to be.

* * * * * *

For the past two days Shitty had been roaming the streets of Baltimore, which is known as body-more. It got its name due to the constant gun violence and being a top 10 murder rate city for the last couple of decades with no sign of slowing down anytime soon.

Shitty and a young dude named RodRod was in a rented silver 2019 Mazda ZR6 with tinted windows. Shitty had met RodRod through RodRod's older cousin Brill, who was his cell mate a couple years back when he was locked up in the feds in West Virginia. Shitty and Brill formed a strong bond being cellmates. Brill had a 25 year sentence when Shitty first met him, and Shitty was about to go home in a year.

Shitty had promised Brill when he got home that he was going to get up with his little cousin RodRod, who kept it all the way 100 with his big cousin on the money tip, visits and whatever else Brill needed him to do. RodRod had called Shitty two days ago and asked him if he could make it out to Baltimore in an hour. He had gotten some information on the whereabouts on a dude by the name of JB.

JB, who's real name is Leon Cougar, is a known rat and had gotten RodRod's big cousin and Shitty's man Brill, 25 years. See, the day before, when Shitty first came to Baltimore to get up on JB, RodRod told him he disappeared before Shitty got the chance to get there. He told him not to leave because he had the girl JB lived with address.

Shitty and RodRod had been laying low at the house where the girl JB stayed with lived on McCabe & Craig Avenue for the last 30 or so hours. They only left one time to go get food and make backwoods to smoke with. This was nothing new to Shitty. He'd done this hundreds of times to get his vicks, but RodRod was tired of waiting, and was ready to go hours ago. Shitty convinced him to stay because he didn't know how JB looked and killing him would help get Brill back home if he got back in court and got a retrial. Shitty was getting tired as well due to all the dro of backwood they had smoked and was now dosing off.

"Bout time!" said RodRod.

"What up slim?" Shitty said waking up out of his daze and looking at RodRod.

"Dat's him pulling up right dere," RodRod yelled excitedly, pointing to a black Audi A4 that was parking in front of their vicks house. Shitty ain't even respond back, he just slowly got out his rented Mazda and walked across the street and straight towards the Audi. JB was just closing his car door and heading to his house when he heard Shitty call out his name.

"Ay, yo name JB?" Shitty asked as he got within three feet of him. He didn't have on a mask and looked like he was about 15 years old, so JB ain't sense any danger whatsoever from the young killer.

"Yea, my name JB! Who da fuck is you tho, yo?" JB asked, looking Shitty up and down with a mean mug on his face.

"Oh, I ain't nobody, slim. I just came by to tell you Brill said what's up!" Shitty said with a smile on his face as he whipped his small Glock 30. 45 from out his sleeve of his Dolce and Gabanna sweatshirt.

As soon as JB heard the name 'Brill' his heart dropped, because he already knew that his time had finally come. Shitty pointed his Glock to JB's chest who was in shock and ain't even try to run. He fired three shots at point blank.

BOP! BOP! BOP!

Shitty fired, hitting JB in his chest and he dropped to the ground with blood oozing from his wounds. He then walked up and stood over him with his Glock pointed at his head. "Dis wat happens to hot niggas." He pulled the trigger of his Glock, firing four more shots in JB's head.

BOP! BOP! BOP! BOP!

The power from the compact Glock 45 knocked fragments of his skull and brains out his head. Shitty turned and ran back to his rented silver Mazda and jumped in the passenger seat since RodRod was now in the driver seat. The car pulled off, tires squealing.

"Now what, yo?" RodRod asked Shitty once they was about three blocks away from the crime scene and waiting at a red light.

"Shit! You could drop yourself off and den I'm going back down to D.C.," Shitty replied wanting to get back to his city and out of Baltimore as quick as possible after just committing a murder.

"Aite, bet," RodRod said nodding.

The light turned green and he drove off heading to his destination. Once RodRod got to where he wanted to go, he and Shitty switched seats. They promised to meet in a few weeks to go party. After some more small talk RodRod finally gave Shitty a dap before getting out the car and headed down the block.

Shitty puts in Lil Durk's new *Love Song 4 The Streets 2'* CD and turned to *'Die Slow'* as he slowly pulled off while bopping his head all the way back to D.C.

CHAPTER 16

"Shy, y'all gonna buy us some food? We hungry," said one of the little thots KGR, Shy, and Loc had.

KGR, Shy and Loc had just came from the studio two hours ago and had been around Saratoga ever since. They'd been outside the whole time trying to get the two thots Tiff and Ashley to let them go in their apartment. The only reason they were over there was because Shy said the two thots were going to let all of them fuck and so far they'd just been playing and teasing which was getting Loc and KGR mad.

Tiff was short at 5'2, one-hundred and twenty-five pounds with a body to kill for. Tiff was brown-skinned with a short haircut. Ashley on the other hand was a bad redbone that was tatted up from her neck on down. She was 5'5, one-hundred and forty-four pounds, and thick.

Shy was getting fed up with them playing games as well and got straight to the point. "Man, Tiff, y'all playing. We ain't come around here to be standing around another nigga's block! We tryna go in the apartment. We could order some Chinese food in there. And then we tryna fuck!" Shy yelled, looking at Tiff.

"Y'all the ones ain't ever say nothing about going in the house, so we thought y'all was coolin'. Come on, we can go in the house," Tiff said and they all entered the building and Tiff's apartment.

"Bout time," Loc said once they got in the apartment and sat on the couch.

The apartment was a two-bedroom and empty other than a 42-inch flat screen TV, a couch in the living room and one mattress on the floor of both bedrooms.

"So, who going to order the carryout?" Ashley looked at KGR.

"Shid, you lookin' at me. You better holla at Shy because if I'm ordering some carryout. We need to be fuckin', right?" KGR said to Ashley dead serious.

"Boy, you ain't got to do all dat. I'm most definitely going to fuck da shit out of your sexy ass," Ashley said, walking up on KGR and sitting on his lap.

"One of y'all can order the food. We'll go get it and pay for it," Shy said to Tiff.

"Go 'head order it, bitch!" Tiff yelled to Ashley as she threw her cell phone.

"A'ight, Bitch," Ashley replied to Tiff as she caught her phone and called the carryout.

Once the carryout answered Ashley asked Shy, KGR and Loc did they want anything and they all said no, so she just ordered her and Tiff's food and hung up. As soon as she hung up the phone KGR grabbed her by her hand and walked her to the back room while he signaled for Loc to follow them. Shy and Tiff stayed and sucked and fucked on the couch.

After about twenty minutes of fuckin' and g'tting' their dicks sucked the carryout called back and said they was out front.

"I got it," Loc said as he put on his coat and left out the apartment to get the food.

Once outside the building Loc saw a light green Dodge Neon double parked in the middle of the street looking in his direction, so he walked to the car.

"You order Chinese food?" The old Chinese lady said in her Chinese accent as Loc walked to the passenger's side window where the food was sitting in the seat.

"Yeah, how much?" Loc asked, looking around inside her car.

"Twenty-one dollar, twenty-cents," The old Chinese lady said, looking at the receipt on the bag of food.

"A'ight," Loc said as he reached for his waist and whipped out his black Glock 26.

"Please no, don't shoot!" The old Chinese lady yelled scared to death.

"Bitch, shut the fuck up and put your hands!" Loc yelled, pointing the Glock at her face and grabbing the bags of food with the other hand.

As Loc was trying to get a good grab of the bags due to it being a couple, the old Chinese lady made a sneaky move to try and put the car in drive, but Loc caught her.

"Bitch if you touch that gear shift, I'ma knock shrimp fried rice out of your ass!" Loc yelled as he grabbed the bag out the car. He pointed the gun at her and told her to get the fuck on and as she hit the gas to drive off Loc ran back to the building.

Once back in the apartment Loc gave Tiff the food and went back in the backroom where KGR and Ashley was still at. When Loc got to the bedroom door, he ain't even go in, he just told Ashley the food was out there, who almost broke her neck to pass him to get it, and called Shy to the back with him and KGR so he could let them know what he just did.

"Ay, y'all we gone. I just robbed the Chinese bitch for dat food. We got to get the fuck cause they got shorty's number and apartment and the police 'bout to blitz dis joint in 'bout five min," Loc said dead serious.

"Slim, we gone! Fuck dem bitches, we already did us," KGR said as him, Shy and Loc headed to leave.

"Where y'all going?" Tiff asked Shy as they headed to the door.

"We just got a call. We gotta get the fuck! Call my phone later," Shy lied as KGR opened the apartment door.

"A'ight, thank you for the food!" Ashley yelled with her mouth full of French fries.

"Dat shit ain't 'bout nothin'," Shy said as they left out the door and jogged to the stolen Honda truck they still had.

As soon as they all got in the truck Loc started it up and pulled off.

"Moe, damn bitches 'bout to go to jail," Shy said, shaking his head as Loc stopped at the stop sign on the corner of the block.

"Dat bitch talkin' 'bout thanks for the food y'all," Loc mocked in a girl like voice. "Dat bitch don't even know dat's 'bout to be her last Chinese food for a brick," KGR said as they all bust out laughing.

Loc made a left and pulled off heading back around their hood, as three police cars made a right heading to the two thots house.

CHAPTER 17

Baby Boy had finally got out of the hospital after being shot a month earlier. Him, Shitty and their crew were down bottom chilling and smoking with Mello, Guala, Fat Marcus and Eroc since they squashed their beef a week ago.

"Moe, I swear to God da next time I catch dat nigga Wally Gator out here off da late night, I'ma smoke his ass!" Shitty yelled to his crew talking about a crackhead that everybody around the Yo' fucked with when they needed a ride or somebody to make a store or food run for them.

"Why da fuck you beefin' wit' Wally Gator, cuz?" Mello asked Shitty.

"Mannnn, my bitch had my car last night right. So, I had dis wild ass nigga take me to get dis lil' bitch, and he was supposed to come back and take her home at eleven before my bitch came back from da bar and his bitch ass ain't never come back," Shitty explained getting mad that Wally Gator played games with him last night. "But dat ain't even what got me so hot. I called dat nigga back at one-thirty in da morning and he said his bad and dat he had sumthin' important to do. He was ready to come outside, Moe. We go outside and he ain't even out dere. So, I called his crackhead ass back and he said he was on his way and to just cool. Dat nigga ain't never come. He had me out dere wit' dat bitch until like two-thirty in da morning. Had me lookin' wild as shit," Shitty continued venting, but even had to laugh thinking back about what happened.

Everybody bust out laughing hard as shit and what we made it even funnier was that Wally Gator did some wild shit to almost everybody right there a time or two.

"So, what happened? Where da bitch at? Because ain't no Ubers at three in da morning," Squirt said to Shitty trying to stop himself from still laughing so hard.

"Slim, she just caught a Uber dis morning," Shitty said laughing. "I had to take her in my grandmova joint and sleep with her on da couch. I still ain't been in da house yet. I been ducking wifey calls all night. I know she mad as shit," Shitty continued shaking his head.

"Kill you playin', Mook gonna fuck you up. You might as well go in da house and take dat ass whippin'!" Baby Boy joked.

"Yeah, I'm already hip, but fuck dat. How you doing? You was in da hospital for a brick I thought your ass was gonna die," Shitty said dead serious.

"Yeah, slim, thanks to Squirt and Lil' E I'm good. Da doctor said if I would've came in dere a minute too late I would've died. I still got bullets in my spine, dey said if dey try to take dem out I could get paralyzed, but I'm good, tho." Baby Boy threw a three-piece of punches at the wind.

"Kill, ain't no secret," Shitty said dapping Baby Boy up.

"Is you and Baby Boy finished y'all moment yet, damn?" Turk joked. "Is everybody goin' to da La Pearl tonight?" Turk continued always geeking to go out and party.

He was talking about a GoGo Club on Central Avenue out Maryland that they go to every Sunday to see TCB.

"No question. You already know dat's mandatory. Matter fact, let's all slide up G-town and grab some Versace and

119

Sergio shit," Mac said to all of them talking about going to Georgetown which is an upscale shopping district in D.C. where mainly white people live and shop.

"Bet, we gone," Mello said as they all headed to their cars to go shopping.

* * * * * *

Later that night Mac, Lips, Day-Day, Fats, Shy, Shitty, Lil E, Loc, Eroc, Squrit, Baby Boy, Turk, KGR and Guala were all in the alley drinking and smoking getting ready to go out. They were all fly as shit wearing Versace, Chanel, Prada and you already know their city's favorite Hugo Boss. Everything was good and everybody was all smiles, but little did any of them know this would be the last time they'd all go out together...*Ever.*

"Ay, who all driving?" Mac asked.

"Shid, we deep as shit! But you, Shitty, Flip and Lips drive everybody else just gonna get in where dey fit in wit' y'all," Squirt said, drinking a cup of Ciroc Pineapple.

"Man, I'm driving, too. I ain't got dat Honda Truck for nothing," Loc said just wanting to drive.

"A'ight, bet," Squirt said not caring.

"A'ight everybody got their dogs on dem?" Flip said, looking around at everybody.

"Is a pig's pussy pink or pork?" Shitty yelled, looking at Flip like he was crazy for asking a stupid question as everybody bust out laughing.

"Say less, we gone den," Mac said, laughing as they all got ready to leave.

As soon as they got in the club, Mac and Bo went to let Polo the lead mic for the band TCB know that 37th was in the building.

"Ay, thirty seventh where da alley at!" Polo said as they walked to the back where the rest of them was at.

"Ay, we 'bout to go buy some bottles and den go to the picture booth," Flip said to his men while walking toward the bar.

"Ay, let us get twenty bottles of Rose Moet," Flip requested from the pretty bartender.

"You said twenty?" she asked, looking at Flip like he was crazy.

"Yeah, it's seventeen of us. So, we all need one and we just grabbing the other ones on the strength, but that's neither here nor dere. Let us get dem so we can do us," Flip said getting irritated.

"Oh, a'ight my bad. I know thirty seventh getting money," she said, laughing already knowing who they were as she walked off to get the bottles two at a time. When she had all twenty bottles on the bar, she said, "That's gonna be thirty-five hundred."

"Say less," Flip said, handing her $3,700. "Dat thirty-seven hundred. Dat way you won't forget about us," Flip said, walking off, leaving her looking stuck and happy that she just got a $200 tip.

They all then went to the picture booth.

"Ay, let us get the rest of the pictures," Sway said when it was their turn, telling the picture man they was buying the booth so nobody else could take pics after them.

"All right, give me eleven-hundred and it's y'alls," the picture man said.

"Bet," Sway said, handing him the money.

As soon as they got in the picture booth, they started having a ball taking the extra bottles of Rose and having a champagne shower. This got the whole club's attention, especially from the bitches when Bo and Lips started throwing money in the air. The whole time the cameraman was snapping pictures non-stop and bitches started rushing the booth picking up money and get drowned in Moet. After causing all the commotion TCB had no choice but to amp the 37th niggas up even more.

So, Polo kicked it off by saying, "Ay, thirty seventh where da alley at, niggas? Ay, thirty seventh take it back, take it back! Ay, they got one-hunnid guns and one-hunnid clips cause they from thirty seventh. Thirty seventh you can tell the way the k spit that they from thirty seventh!" Polo rapped on the mic getting the 37th niggas hyped up in the picture booth.

Turk and Mello were in the booth beating their feet while everybody else was hyping them up and throwing their hands up to the GoGo band stamping their hood. While the 37th niggas were having the time of their lives. The Paradise niggas that they were beefing with were looking and hating. But in true GoGo fashion as soon as they stopped stamping 37th they started stamping the niggas they was beefing with.

"Ay, Paradise got that ice!" Polo started rapping in the mic getting the Paradise niggas amped up, too.

E-roc who's always with the bullshit started walking toward the Paradise niggas dancing wild and all the 37th niggas were right behind him with one thing on their mind, work. They all started dancing wildly by the Paradise niggas until Eroc bumped one of them.

"Da fuck y'all niggas doing?" the tall, dark-skinned nigga from Paradise said to Eroc.

Before Eroc could reply Mello popped off on the dark-skinned dude and all hell broke loose for The 37th dudes and it showed because they were all over them whooping their ass until the bouncers broke it up and threw them out.

"Ay, Loc let me see da keys to da Honda truck and you drive my three-hunnid," Shitty said trying get some highway action.

"A'ight, bet here," Loc said swapping keys and ran to Shitty car with KGR.

"Ay, Squirt grab my Mac and you and Day-Day hop in dere with me. So, we can slide around dere, right now and fuck dat joint up," Shitty said as the rest of the 37th niggas ran to get into the cars they came in.

"A'ight, bet," Squirt said running to get the Mac out of Shitty's car before Loc pulled off.

"Man, how y'all gonna leave us without a dog. KGR's dog in the truck with y'all!" Loc yelled mad at Squirt.

"Man, we 'bout to slide. Y'all gonna be a'ight, you know how to drive," Squirt said running off with the Mac tucked so P.G Police couldn't see it and hopping in the backseat of the Honda truck since Squirt was already up front.

Before the door closed all the way Shitty was pulling off. He made the left out of the club parking lot onto East Capital and hit it not stopping at no lights because after the GoGo that was a no-no unless you wanted your car swiss cheesed. As they approached the light by Capitol Heights Station, Day-Day spotted a familiar car about to make a right turn toward Watts and 58th Northeast.

"Ay slim dat's dem niggas from Paradise right dere in that blue Park Avenue dey be driving all da time, Kill," Day-Day said getting Squirt and Shitty's attention.

"Oh, dat's definitely dem. Shitty get up on dat joint," Squirt said checking the Mac-10 making sure there was one in the head and that it was off safety.

"I got dis, bra. Y'all just be ready, Moe," Shitty said gaining on the car, but not making it obvious.

"Man, we ready dis shit ain't nothin' new," Day-Day said, holding KGR's Glock .27 and rolling his window down.

The car was now headed toward Sherriff Road in Northeast obviously they thought they was in the clear because they made a fatal error and broke a #1 D.C. rule never stop at a light after the club no matter what! As the car stopped at the light Shitty pulled up on the driver's side and stopped. Squirt was already hanging out the window with the Mac-10 in his hand and a smirk on his face as he and Day-Day started shooting.

Bok! Bok! Bok!

Boom! Boom! Boom! Boom!

Bok! Bok!

The guns sounded off like that for an eternity it seemed before Shitty finally pulled off while Park Avenue was drifting off slowly with its occupants shot all up and dying!

CHAPTER 18

It was 6 o'clock in the evening and Mello was sitting in the parking lot in front of Guala's house waiting for him. Mello had just gotten off the phone with Shitty, they had finally come up with a plan to punish Guala for his disloyalty to Leeky and Down bottom. Mello had just got off the phone with Guala right before he called Shitty and told him that he needed him to ride with him over some bitch's house.

"What's up, bra? Who da fuck car is dis?" Guala said as he opened the stolen car door of an all-white 2019 Audi A4, that Lil' E and Sway had just carjacked somebody for out Virginia an hour earlier.

"Dis one of my lil' bitches joint. But what it do, bra?" Mello replied to Guala keeping him in the dark and giving him dap as he got all the way in the car and shut the door.

"I'm not on shit. I was 'bout to call my lil' old head bitch and go fuck wit' her before you called," Guala said as Mello pulled off.

"Oh, yeah, you could've went and fuck wit' her for real. I could've called Eroc or Fat Marcus to ride wit' me," Mello said playing it off like he ain't really care if Guala rode with him or not.

"Nah, bra fuck dat bitch. You already know I don't break my neck for no bitch. But anyway, where da fuck dese bitches live at?" Guala asked Mello.

"Dey live uptown around C.T.U.," Mello said.

"Oh, yeah, I ain't had no uptown bitch before," Guala confessed excited that he was about to finally get some uptown pussy.

"Dat's crazy, slim. Dese bitches we 'bout to go fuck wit' bad as shit," Mello said really amping Guala up and keeping the blind on his eyes.

"Say less," Guala said, getting comfortable in his seat knowing they was about to drive at least twenty minutes from where they were to get to C.T.U. in Northwest, D.C. "You already know dat's law wit' me," Guala said, pulling out a chrome and black Kimber 45.

"We good den," Mello said as he put in *Lil Baby's* new CD *My Turn In* the CD player and turned it up to the max after putting it on the song *Woah* and headed uptown.

* * * * * *

Twenty Minutes Later

Mello and Guala pulled up around C.T.U. just as it was getting dark. Mello parked behind a gold Honda as he and Guala got out and headed inside the building a few feet away from them. Mello went into the building, jogged up a couple steps and went straight into an apartment without knocking with Guala right behind him. As soon as Guala closed the door and locked it out of the blue Mello whipped out a Glock 23. on him.

"Holddd!" Guala said off guard, but at the same time reaching for his gun.

126

"Man, put your motherfuckin' hands up for I smoke your ass!" Mello yelled at Guala with his Glock pointed at him as he did just that.

"What's up, bra? What da fuck I do?" Guala said scared to death.

"You know what da fuck your snake ass did," Shitty said appearing out of the kitchen with another dude Guala had never seen before.

Shitty was with his man Moochie from C.T.U. who help him set the whole play up for Guala. Moochie was 6'1, two-hundred pounds with a long beard like most the whole D.C. due to him being Muslim. Shitty met Moochie locked up years ago over D.C. jail and they bonded tight and it stayed that way even after they were released like the real do.

When Mello had called Shitty earlier, he was uptown with Moochie, and Mello told Shitty he was ready to back door Guala. Shitty told him to bring him uptown and texted Mello the directions and the apartment door number. When Guala saw Shitty's face, he already knew he was a dead man and for the first time he finally looked around the apartment and noticed it was a vacant unit.

Guala looked up at Mello with tears in his eyes and started pleading for his life. "Bra, please don't kill me, Moe. I swear I never snaked you out, bra!"

"Don't trip, bra, I ain't even gonna kill you." Mello was saying as Moochie crept on the side of Guala with a 357 Bulldog Revolver, lifted it to his head and pulled the trigger.

Boom! Boom!

Hitting him twice in the head, knocking the whole right side of his brain and skull off as he hit the floor with a loud thump. As soon as Guala hit the floor and now lifeless, Shitty pulled out his Glock 30 and shot him three more times in his face just for the hell of it.

"Bra we gone," Shitty said to Mello after he unlocked the vacant door to leave.

"Ay, good lookin', bra! I'ma hit you later," Shitty said to Moochie as he and Mello dapped Moochie up and headed out of the building.

Once outside the building Shitty and Mello jogged a block over leaving the stolen Audi A4 that Mello drove, and jumping in the back of Shitty's blue 300c with Mari waiting behind the wheel. As soon as Shitty and Mello was in the car Mari pulled off heading back around the Yo.

CHAPTER 19

The day after Guala got killed, down bottom was live and people that hadn't been seen in a minute popped up trying to figure out what was going on. It had been less than two months and Leeky and Guala had both gotten killed. It had the whole Down Bottom shook, but Mello. Mello, Mari, Nine, Lil E, Loc and KGR were on the frontline by the ice cream truck that usually sits Down Bottom and never moves just cooling drinking on Rose Moet talking shit.

"Y'all youngins funny as shit, Kill," Mello said, laughing at KGR and Nine.

"Nah, for real dis wild nigga KGR gonna throw the lil bitches out the trap last night because da lil bitch said she was on her period," Nine said.

"Dis nigga ain't even wait till I fucked da lil bitch I had or nothin. He put both of dem bitches out," Nine continued still laughing.

Nine was from Down Bottom and hangs with Mari, KGR and Loc. Nine was a young nigga just like them. He was seventeen-years-old, 5'9, one-hundred and sixty-five pounds and brown-skinned with a beard. Shitty and his crew in the alley fucked with Nine hard as well because shorty would shoot his gun without a second thought at whoever and on top of that he was from the Yo and fucked with KGR, Mari and Loc heavy.

"Damn, he ain't let you get no pussy? I know you ain't go like dat, Nine?" Lil E said, trying to amp Nine to get into it with KGR.

"You already know I ain't goin' for nothin' like dat, and KGR knows dat. Dis wild nigga waited till I ran to go get some loud from Sway in the circle and den put dem bitches out," Nine said shaking his head.

"Fuck dem bitches. Dey was playing games," KGR said, picking up the bottle of Rose and taking a sip.

"Man, what da fuck up wit' y'all niggas?" Squirt said as he walked up.

"Shit, where da fuck you just come from? A nigga ain't even see you walk up," Mello said as him and everybody gave Squirt dap.

"Dat's cause y'all right here drunk and lackin' like shit. But nah, I just parked behind the ice cream truck and walked right here," Squirt said smiling.

"Yeah, we most definitely not lackin' it's at least one hundred, right here," Loc said fucking with Squirt, but at the same time dead serious.

"Yeah, y'all bet not be lacki..." Squirt was saying when all of a sudden a black caravan pulled up and two dudes in all black jumped out with AK-47s firing in their direction.

Doom! Doom! Doom! Doom! Doom! Doom!

Both gunmen fired at the same time with nothing but murder on their minds.

"Bra, watch out!" Loc said to KGR who had his back turned toward the street as him, Nine, Mari and Mello all whipped out their guns ready to return fire.

Loc's warning was a little too late as the gunmen's first couple of shots hit KGR in his back and right shoulder and spun him around before he fell face first to the pavement dying.

Bok! Bok! Bok! Bok! Bok! Bok!

Loc fired his Glock .26 at the two gunmen in all black as he saw his righthand man hit the ground. As Loc started shooting so did everybody else, except Squirt. Squirt ain't have his gun on him, so as Loc and the rest of his current crew exchange shots Squirt ran to his Camaro and grabbed the Draco that he'd just traded two Glocks and $500 for an hour ago. Squirt grabbed the Draco and ran back to assist his men as quick as possible.

"Y'all watch out, bra," Squirt said to Lil E and Mari as he came up behind them with his Draco in hand. "Niggas wanna bring out choppers, I got something for dey ass!" Squirt said as he began firing his Draco.

Cock! Cock! Cock! Cock! Cock! Cock! Cock! Cock! Cock! Cock! Cock! Cock!

Squirt fired while at the same time Nine and Loc were still firing their Glocks causing the two gunmen to fire a couple of more shots before jumping back in their caravan and speeding off.

After the unknown shooters jumped back in the caravan and tried to speed off, that ain't stop Squirt, Loc and the rest of their current crew from trying to kill them. Squirt and Lil' E ran in the middle of the street and continued shooting their guns while Mello and Nine stayed off the sidewalk and continued firing. Loc tried his best to run the caravan down firing his Glock .26 furiously in anger that his righthand man been shot.

After the caravan was gone, everybody hurried to check on KGR. KGR was lying by the front wheels of the ice cream truck with no signs of life. His eyes were wide open, but he wasn't breathing.

When Squirt saw his lil' brother on the ground dead, he yelled, *"Fuckkk!"* He closed his eyes and started walking to his car with his Draco still in hand.

It was so many people outside down bottom and witnesses to the whole shooting. Besides KGR getting killed, a man named Bo, that everyone called 'Uncle Bo' and owned the ice cream truck, was shot in his left arm while he sat in his truck during the shootout. Also, a girl named, Sunshine was shot in her face as a bullet went through her apartment building window while she was looking at TV, and a man named, Lu-Lu got shot twice in his chest and died as he tried to run toward the shootout with his Ruger P.89 in hand to aid and assist his men.

"Moe, we got to put dese dogs up and get the fuck before dem people pull up!" Mari yelled to Mello, Lil' E, Loc and Nine who were all staring at KGR's dead body in shock. "Ain't no secret, let's go put dese joints in YaYa's house," Mello said.

"I'm 'bout to go holla at Squirt. I'ma see y'all later," Lil' E said as Mello, Mari and Nine walked off to YaYa's house why he walked to Squirt's car with Loc right behind him.

Squirt was on the phone with his mother crying, letting her know that KGR had just got killed around 37th. As soon as Lil' E and Loc got in Squirt's Camaro he finished his call and started up the car ready to pull off.

"You good, bra?" Lil' E asked Squirt as they pulled off.

"Yeah, slim, dis shit wild! Where da fuck Shitty and Day-Day?" Squirt said, shaking his head wiping the tears from his eyes with his left hand while he drove with his right hand.

"I don't know, I'm 'bout to hit dem," Lil' E said, pulling out his iPhone 10 to try to call Shitty and Day-Day.

"Loc you good, bra?" Squirt said, looking in his rearview mirror at Loc, who hadn't said a word since KGR got killed.

Loc had his head down with his Glock still in his hand, reminiscing about his right-hand man. KGR's death hurt Loc more than anybody. They were Thing-1 and Thing-2, off the movie *Cat in the Hat*, they were rarely apart and it's been like that for years.

"Nah, bra. I'm ready to fuck dis whole city up. I'm 'bout to paint dis motherfucker red, watch!" Loc yelled to Squirt without lifting his head or looking at Squirt.

"You already know dat, lil bra," Squirt replied.

"Did dem niggas answer?" Squirt asked Lil' E who still had his cell phone to his ear but wasn't talking.

"Nah, I don't know what the fuck is up wit' dem niggas," Lil' E said shaking his head.

"Don't worry 'bout it. Dem niggas gonna call back fast when they hear 'bout what happened. But we got to find out who the fuck was dat," Squirt said as he made a right turn leaving 37th heading down Double R trying to see if Turk or Baby Boy had heard who'd just came around the Yo' shooting and killed his lil brother.

* * * * * *

"I know dem niggas ain't think shit was sweet," said one of the gunmen that just was involved in the shooting with Squirt and his crew.

The gunmen name was Fatface, he was from a hood uptown D.C. called 17th Street. He was with his cousin that was from 34th named, Kool-Aid that Loc and KGR shot and robbed and took the Honda truck from. Kool-Aid ain't have no idea where the young niggas were from that shot him and took his car a month ago, until an hour earlier when he happened to go meet an old head dude named T.R. up 37th in the circle and just happened to see KGR and Loc down bottom chilling as he rode past, heading back around 34th. As soon as Kool-Aid saw them, he called his lil' cousin Fatface and told him he'd found out who shot and robbed him.

"Yeah, lil' cuz, fuck dem niggas. I bet you dey won't rob without facemasks no more," Kool-Aid said taking off his facemask.

"Ain't no secret, I know I crashed the lil' light-skinned nigga off the break," Fatface said talking about KGR.

"Dat chopper spun shorty's lil' ass," Fatface said laughing.

"Yeah, I was tryna punish both of dem lil' niggas. We ain't get da one who hit me tho," Kool-Aid said. "But fuck dat shit now. I'm good, but if I ever catch that lil' nigga lackin', I'ma crush his ass."

"Yeah, I hear you big cuz. But y'all can take me back uptown," Fatface said not trying to stay around 34th after the shootout.

"Say less, we gone! Drop dese guns off," Kool-Aid said to Fatface.

"Bet," Fatface agreed as they turned down 34th to drop the guns off, then jumped in a different car and head uptown.

CHAPTER 20

Three Days Later

After KGR was killed Shitty and his whole crew except Loc was in the alley still trying to figure out who killed KGR but couldn't come up with nothing due to all the beef they had around the city. The day before Shitty and his crew went through three different hoods that they had beef with shooting just because they couldn't figure out which one might have shot they hood up and killed KGR. Today they were on the same mission to go paint the city red like Loc promised.

"Ay, we fucked up Simp, Paradise and Parkland yesterday. So, what we goin' around 55th and Clay Terrace today?" Lil E said to his crew smiling.

"Yeah, we 'bout to go around dere soon after Loc and Mari come back wit' a U.U." Squirt said smoking on some Purple Haze.

"Man, fuck da. What time is it?" Shitty asked Day-Day.

"It's five-thirteen!" Day-Day yelled as he passed him the blunt of dro.

"A'ight, dat's a bet," Shitty said. "Look, Sway, got to take the BMW truck back at six-thirty. So, we can go through in dat. Den he can take dat joint back, we got a whole hour."

"Bet, we gone. We ain't shootin' out no cars anyway," Squirt informed ready to go.

"Say less," Day-Day said.

"But all us don't need to go! Look, you, Shitty and Squirt go round Clay and when Loc and Mari come back me, Lil E, Sway and Loc gonna fuck up fifty-fifth," Flip said to Day-Day agreeing that seven of them in the BMW truck would be too deep and if seen by the police they would most definitely get pulled over.

"Ay, bet. Sway let me see dem keys to the X-six," Shitty said. Sway threw him the keys to the BMW truck. "We gone!" Shitty yelled walking to the BMW truck that was parked a few feet away from them and behind his 300c with Squirt and Day-Day not far behind him. As Shitty got to the driver's side door of the BMW he stopped and called to Flip

"Ay, Flip if Nine comes up here lookin' for me tell him dat glizzy in the trap where it's always at and give him dese keys. Tell him to go get Shy from the studio," Shitty said, forgetting he had to go pick Shy up and throwing him his keys to his 300c before getting in the BMW truck and pulling off.

* * * * * *

Ten Minutes Later

Shitty was driving in the 2019 white X6 BMW truck blasting *Lil' Wayne's* new album *Tha Carter 5* with Day-Day and Squirt. They had just turned off East Capitol and was now coming down Division Avenue heading to Clay Terrace hoping to catch their vicks slipping.

"Bra, Lil Wayne is back, Kill. Him and Kendrick fucked dis joint up," Day-Day said to Shitty bopping his head to *Lil Wayne* and *Kendrick Lamar's* song *Mona Lisa.*

"Nah, for real. Dis whole CD hard as shit," Shitty said, bopping his head hard as well.

"Ay, Moe, dis nigga Shy fuckin' a nigga phone up. I bet dis nigga don't want nothin'," Squirt said to Shitty looking at the iPhone, not answering Shy's call as they made the second to last right turn off division Avenue on a street that led them to Clay Terrace.

The street they turned on didn't only lead to Clay Terrace, but it led to a part where everybody hangs out called Briscoe Court. Shitty drove all the way to the end of the street, he turned on and stopped at the stop sign at the end of the corner.

"Moe, Shy keep callin' my joint, too. Dat nigga Nine must ain't go pick dat nigga up yet," Shitty said, looking at his iPhone 10 ignoring Shy's call. "I'll call dat nigga when we finish. But look I'ma sit right here while y'all do y'all. Cause I'm not 'bout to ride pass den drive back through because dey be playin' hot D," Shitty said, throwing the truck in park, not turning in off.

"Say less," Day-Day said as he and Squirt got out of the truck with Murder on their minds.

Day-Day had his all black Glock 30 tucked under his grey Star hoodie, while Squirt had his Draco hid behind his back and they walked across to Briscoe Court. Once across the street Squirt and Day-Day spotted their vicks. They saw two dudes named Pitch and Rah standing with their backs turned with an old head dude named Scooter. They were chilling and smoking on PCP that Squirt and Day-Day smelled as soon as they exited their truck and crossed the street. They weren't paying no attention to what was going on around them at all. They were so high they ain't even notice Squirt and Day-Day creeping up on them.

Once directly behind them Day-Day shot Rah twice in the back of his head, killing him instantly and he fell face first to the ground.

Pitch and Scooter jumped so hard when they heard the loud bang from Day-Day's 45 Glock that Squirt had to stop from laughing. Pitch and Scooter, now in shock and slightly sober, turned around and looked in front of them with guns in hand.

"What's up wit' y'all youngins?" Scooter said not knowing who Squirt and Day-Day were from being twenty-years-older and not involved in their beef or any other beefs for that matter.

Pitch was just standing there looking at Squirt and Day-Day in a daze already knowing his fate was sealed. Pitch was one of the main dudes around Clay Terrace that they'd been beefing with and trying to kill for about a year.

"You already know we ain't come to talk," Squirt said as he lifted his Draco up at Pitch and looked him in the eyes before pulling the trigger.

Doom! Doom! Doom! Doom! Doom!

Squirt fired four times hitting Pitch in his face and chest, knocking the front of his face off as the power from the Draco threw him to a ground a couple of feet farther back. As soon as Squirt fired his first shot form the Draco, Day-Day followed suit hitting Scooter three times in his chest, dropping him to the ground then feeding him five more bullets in his head and face.

"Bra, we gone," Squirt said, looking at Day-Day before jogging off heading back to Shitty in the waiting BMW truck.

"A'ight, I'm right," Day-Day said. "You bitch ass nigga!"

Bok! Bok! Bok!

Day-Day pointed his Glock at an already dead Pitch and fired three more shots in his body before running and getting in the truck with Shitty and Squirt. Shitty pulled off, headed back around the Yo.

CHAPTER 21

"YoYo," Shy said, walking in Shitty's girl Mook's house down Stoneridge, giving him dap.

Shitty had been in the house with his girl Mook all day, having sex and looking at movies. Shy called Shitty when he pulled up around the Yo in the alley and nobody was out there which was unusual. Shitty told him to come down Stoneridge to Mook's house and fuck with him. Shitty hadn't seen Shy in almost two weeks. Shy had been falling back on playing da alley and was focusing more on his music. He'd been hitting the studio up night in and night out, he'd just got finished dropping his new mixtape, *How I'm Comin'*, and had the streets on lock. Shy was the hottest artist in the DMV area hands down and was on the rise to becoming a real rap star.

"YoYo, what it do, bra? Where the fuck you been?" Shitty asked as Shy sat next to him on the couch.

"You already know. I been fuckin' dat studio up tryna give us a different way to get a bag because dis street shit can't last forever," Shy said looking Shitty in his eyes, dead serious.

"Nigga I hear you, but since you got all over Leeky you been ghost," Shitty said. "You must been having dreams about dat shit," Shitty continued trying to bid off Shy who couldn't help but laugh.

That was most definitely part of the reason Shy was laying low in the studio more often. That's why he had to laugh since he caught his first body on Leeky. Everyday Shy saw a police car around the Yo, he felt that the police was going to grab him for Leeky's murder. So, he'd just been fallin' back.

"Hey, Shy," Mook said coming in the front room with a pink Chanel T-shirt, some pink and lime-green boy shorts and some matching Chanel open toe sandals on.

Mook was looking super fat in her boy shorts and she ain't have on no panties and her boy shorts that were hugging on her so tight you could see her fat pussy trying to bust out the front of her shorts. Mook came in the living room and sat right in Shitty's lap trying to be seen and at the same time trying to be nosy.

"What's up, Mook?" Shy tried to keep his eyes from looking at Mook's pussy print that was hard to miss or not look at especially since she sat down right in front of him.

Unlike other niggas Shitty ain't mind his girl walking around half naked or in super tight shit showing off her goodies, it was *bros over hoes* with him and if she fucked around or cheated he'd just be on to the next. On top of that, he loved seeing his bitch looking super sexy. Shitty saw Shy trying his best not to look at his girl's fat pussy print and busted out laughing.

"Dis joint fat as shit, ain't it, bruh?" Shitty said to Shy putting his hands around Mook, gripping her pussy print through her boy shorts.

"Cut it out, bra! You wild as shit, Kill," Shy said with a slight laugh, shaking his head. "I'm gone." Shy got up from the couch.

"Now why the fuck would you do dat? You so disrespectful," Mook said to Shitty punching him in his chest and getting off his lap, going back into her bedroom with an attitude, slightly embarrassed.

Shitty just brushed her attitude off and turned his attention back to Shy. "Hold, Moe, let me holla at you 'bout sumthin'," Shitty said.

Shy sat back down feeling a little more comfortable now that Mook was gone back in the room. "What it do, bra?" Shy said, looking at Shitty.

"You jy like been ghost. I know you fuckin' wit' dat rap shit hard, but you got to make sure you stay on point. Cause we been sliding thru fuckin' shit up since KGR got hit. And you be doin' shows and shit. Your name ringing on being next to blow from da city. So, you know niggas will love to put dat Draco on you just to get a name," Shitty said to Shy giving him a heads up and making sure he stayed on point so he wouldn't become an easy vick for their opps.

"I appreciate da heads up, bra, for real. You already know I'm hip. Dat's why I keep da glizzy on me no matter where I'm at, kill," Shy said with all seriousness lifting up his shirt showing Shitty the handle of his Glock 17 which had a standard clip inside it.

Shitty seeing Shy without a 30 clip in his gun threw him off because every gun they had had a 21 or 30 shot clip in them.

"Yeah, dats law, I see you straight. But where's your thirty at?" Shitty said.

"I took dat joint out and put da standard back in because dat joint be drawin', stickin' out and shit, kill," Shy said with a slight laugh.

"Oh, yeah, say less. But I'ma let you go head. I know you geekin' to go to da studio and shit," Shitty said. "Make sure you hit my phone later on tho. I'm 'bout to get in da shower and get dressed, then take her over her mova house, den go outside," Shitty continued as he dapped Shy up and walked him to the door.

"A'ight, bet. Love for Life," Shy said as he left out the door.

"Love for Life, Bra!" Shitty yelled to Shy as he closed the door behind him and went in the bedroom with Mook and fucked her brains out before getting in the shower.

"Damn, dis nigga need to hurry da fuck up," Lil' E said to himself, looking at what time it was on his iPhone 10 screen.

It was 11:15 at night and he was standing in the rain in the alley waiting for his brother Shitty to pull back up so he could take him over to his girl house to get some more drugs. Lil' E had just left out the trap after being in there since 10:00 that morning and selling out the whole 125 grams of coke he had brought out, selling only grams for $50 and $20 bags. As Lil' E waited, Fats pulled up down the street in front of his baby mother's house in his black two door Tahoe. Lil' E knew that when it's raining outside Fats usually gonna to just sit in his truck down the street away from the alley and serve crackheads out of his truck.

Lil E said to himself, "I should kill dat fat bitch nigga right now for what he pulled," he said, thinking about how Fats put money on his brother Shitty and Squirt's heads. "Yeah, fuck dat, I'm 'bout to crash his ass," Lil E said as he started walking to the back cut and putting his face mask on.

As soon as Lil' E was walking to the back cut in the alley Shitty was walking out the cut smoking on some loud.

"You ready I parked in the circle," Shitty said soon as he saw his little brother.

"Yeah, but dat's crazy. I was just about to get all over Fats scared ass. He in front of R.D. grandmother's joint right now in the truck, lackin'," Lil' E said.

"Oh, yeah?" Shitty said getting excited.

"Come on. We still 'bout to get all over him," Shitty continued as he pulled his Helly Hanson hood from his jacket over his head and his face mask on.

Lil E did the same, Shitty and Lil E walked through the cut and came out of a cut that was directly across from where Fats was parked. Fats was in the truck eating McDonald's and talking on his cell phone when Shitty came to his driver's side window. Without warning, he fired two shots from the Glock 27 Lil' E gave him breaking the window and hitting him on the side of the face once, but not killing him. Lil' E came up on Fats' passenger side window as planned with Shitty's Mac-10 and started firing recklessly.

Blat! Blat Blat! Blat! Blat! Blat! Blat! Blat!

Lil' E fired, hitting Fats in his head, face, and body, leaving him dead and full of holes. He and Shitty ran back through the cut they came out, took their masks off and started walking like nothing had happened. They walked to the circle, jumped in Shitty car, and pulled off heading to Lil' E girl's house.

CHAPTER 22

"Loc, what's up? We still gonna do dat?" Mari said eatin' a bag of plain UTZ chips.

Mari and Loc were up the yo in the circle sitting on somebody's blue Ford Focus chilling. Mari had been trying to get Loc to rob an older dude named, Funk for the past two days, but Loc had been so stressed out about his right-hand man KGR getting killed that every chance he got he was shooting somebody's hood up. Mari and Funk had gotten into an argument over a dice game two days ago because Funk tried to cheat him. Funk gated the dice late on Mari who was already losing, and from there they got in each other's faces about to fight before someone broke them apart and they went their opposite ways.

Funk is 6 ft, 200 lbs, brown skinned and will remind you of Charlie Murphy. Funk is 40 yrs old and old enough to be Mari and Loc father, but that aint mean nothing to either one of them, they aint have no picks.

"Damn, you geekin' like shit, bra! Where dat nigga at?" Loc said, jumping off the Ford Focus clutching his gun in his wrist.

"His bitch ass right dere wit' big nose Jimmy in the cut," Mari said, jumping off the car as well pointing at Funk and Big Nose Jimmy in the cut behind them.

"Come on," Loc said, walking off toward the cut.

Funk and Big Nose Jimmy were in the cut smoking two fat blunts of weed just enjoying the nice day outside, making small talk when Loc and Mari walked up on them.

"What's up wit' y'all?" Loc said dapping up Funk and Big Nose Jimmy.

"Shit," They both replied, puffing back on their blunts.

"Oh, yeah, dats what's up," Loc said, whipping his Glock 26 out.

Mari followed suit whipping out a chrome and black P.12 Sauer 40. Caught off guard and surprised by Loc and Mari actions Big Nose Jimmy put his hand up and dropped his blunt out of his mouth, Funk on the other hand just mean mugged the youngins and kept smoking his blunt not taking them serious.

"Oh, you think dis shit a game, huh?" Mari asked Funk smiling as he shot him twice in his left shoulder.

Bloc! Bloc! Funk grabbed his shoulder still not fearing them and started talking shit. "Y'all youngins better kill me. Y'all already know what it is," Funk was talking tough and dead serious.

"Nobody worried about your bitch ass. You know what's up wit' da Alley," Loc said as he started going in Funk's pockets pulling out a nice knot of money.

"Nose, you already know what time it is." Mari pointed his gun at Big Nose Jimmy's face.

"What I do, sir?" Big Nose Jimmy asked with fear in his eyes.

"You ain't do nothin'. You was just in da wrong place at da wrong time, sir," Mari mimicked him. "Ballarina," Mari said to Big Nose Jimmy after going in his front pocket.

"What?" Big Nose Jimmy asked confused.

"Ballerina! Dat means spin your bitch ass around!" Mari yelled as he grabbed Big Nose Jimmy by his shoulder and spun him around, checking his back pockets.

After Loc and Mari shot Funk and finished robbing Big Nose Jimmy. They ain't even run, they just walked off heading to the alley. As they were walking down the steps that led to the alley from the top of the hill they saw Flip and Mello.

"Where da fuck y'all comin' from?" Flip asked Loc and Mari as they got to the alley.

"We just got finished bagging Funk and Big Nose Jimmy ugly asses. And Mari hit Funk twice," Loc said, laughing as he dapped him and Mello up.

"What? Man, y'all lunchin'. Y'all 'bout to start a whole nother beef," Flip said shaking his head.

"Fuck dem bitch ass niggas. Dat nigga Funk tried to work me at the crap game the other day," Mari expressed ready to beef with Funk if they wanted beef.

"See y'all youngins don't see nothin'. Dat's what's wrong wit' y'all," Mello said.

"Look, I'm not tryna hear dat shit!" Loc yelled as he and Mari walked off to the back door of the trap and went inside to chill, leaving Flip and Mello just standing there in da alley shaking their head.

● ● ● ● ● ●

Three Hours Later

Mello and Flip was still in the alley with Fat Marcus just cooling smoking and talking shit. They were so much in the zone that they ain't see Funk with his left arm in a sling and his lil' brother Tick walking down the steps guns in hand.

Tick was Funk's identical twin brother, they were only three minutes apart. If you ain't know them for years, it was no way to tell who from who. Funk had a silver 357 Magnum Revolver in his right hand and Tick had an all-black 8 shot Colt 45 in his right hand. As Funk and Tick walked down the last flight of steps before just getting right up on Flip, Mello and Fat Marcus. Fat Marcus saw them and yelled out to Flip and Mello before whipping out his two tone Smith & Wesson 40. Before Fat Marcus got to fully whip out, Funk started firing his 357.

Boom! Boom! Boom! Boom! While at the same time his brother, Tick started firing as well. *Bok! Bok! Bok! Bok! Bok!*

Mello and Flip tried to run as Fat Marcus pulled out the Smith &Wesson 40 and began firing back, but Flip was hit with two shots from Tick Colt 45 in his left side and once in the back by Funk's 357 as he tried to run to the back door of the trap falling face first to the ground. When Funk saw Flip fall face first, he yelled to his brother to come on as they both ran back up the steps and out of sight. As they ran off Fat Marcus fired the last seven of his thirteen shots at them.

Pop! Pop! Pop! Pop! Pop! Pop! Pop!

He ran to Mello's side to help Flip. Upon seeing Mello trying to pick up Flip, Fat Marcus said, "Moe, he fucked over, bra! He needs an ambulance." He pulled out his phone to call for help.

"Look, bra, I'm gone. You good? Dem people on their way. I got to put dis joint up," Fat Marcus said as he shook his head.

He let Fat Marcus know he was good, not having the strength to say it from the pain he was feeling. Fat Marcus ran off, leaving Mello with Flip until the ambulance finally came and took him to the hospital.

CHAPTER 23

Two Days Later

After Flip got shot it seemed like Funk and his brother, Tick disappeared off the face of the earth. Shitty and his crew had been in the circle where they hung at day and night trying to get up on them for shooting Flip. Flip was currently in critical condition in Howard University Hospital. Mello even shot Funk's young flunky Big Nose Jimmy in the ass and pistol whipped him trying to bring Funk out of hiding, but that shit ain't work

"Man, shit been crazy. We got to hit a move and fall back for a minute before all of us be over in the jail," Sway advised his crew.

Shitty, Squirt, Day-Day, Lil E, Loc and Sway were in the trap sitting on the sofa waiting to catch coke and some weed sells and cooling. They'd been inside all day due to the police being constantly parked in their alley because of the large amount of shooting that had been happening around the Yo. On top of, Flip being shot two days ago, two hoods they'd been beefin' with, Simple City and Clay Terrace had been sliding through firing shots as well which between both of them caused four innocent people to be shot. So Shitty and his crew were ducked off in the trap.

"Yeah, you ain't ever lied 'bout dat. But I don't got a move for us," Squirt said talking to his whole crew. "What it do, let's go! Where it's at?"

"Nigga you need to fall back. You and Mari lil' asses already got Flip shot. For now on, y'all youngins need to use a mask. That's going to be y'all down fall watch," Lil' E said to his lil' brother Loc, giving him law.

"Man, whatever!" Loc yelled not giving a fuck about what Lil' E was talking about because he was going to do him regardless.

Knowing both of his little brother's Shitty switched the subject before they started fighting.

"Fuck what dey on. What's up wit' dat move?" Shitty yelled stopping his little brother from getting into it.

"Man, my cousin got a man out in Landover he be buying pounds from. He says he sweet. He tryna set it up for us, it should be a go in 'bout a week," Squirt said to Shitty and the rest of his crew who were wishing they could hit the move today.

"Dat's a bet! Hopefully, we can hit for something cool and go out to Miami or something and fall back," Shitty said as Day-Day passed him a blunt of Sound Diesel he'd just sparked up.

"Ain't no secret," Squirt replied as he got up from the sofa. "I'm 'bout to go holla at Mello right quick. I'll be back," Squirt said, walking out the living room, through the kitchen and leaving out the back door due to the police being parked out front.

As Squirt left out the back door of the trap he began walking up the steps heading down Double R to holla at Mello and Turk when he heard Shitty calling his name. Shitty had just left out the back door of the trap as well and was jogging to catch up with Squirt.

"Your fat ass walks fast as shit," Shitty said as he got up on Squirt.

"Nigga fuck you," Squirt said.

"Nah, for real, bra I got to holla at you on some real shit," Shitty said serious.

Squirt looked at Shitty knowing when he was serious he stopped walking and said, "What's up, bra?"

"Man, you heard about dat nigga Lips telling on da nigga Ram?" Shitty asked shaking his head.

"Yeah, Slim, I saw da paperwork on the gram and everything," Squirt said still in disbelief.

"Man dis why dat nigga ain't been comin' around lately. And Day-Day cut him off, but Sway be with dat nigga every day. I know dat's dey brother, but dat nigga hot. And if dey fuck wit' him, dey condoning dat shit," Shitty said getting mad.

"Yeah, I feel you, but what you think dey gonna do? Dat's dey blood," Squirt said, shaking his head.

"I hear you, but dis all I'm saying. If they fuck wit' Lips hard and dey know he's hot dey might tell. We be doing too much shit to chance it. And you saw how scared Sway looked when he said we gotta fall back before we be over da jail. Dat nigga will tell sumthin'," Shitty said.

"It sounds like you wanna get all over Sway?" Squirt said not really feeling where he was coming from but saw a little bit of what he was talking 'bout.

"On da strength of Day-Day, I'ma give him a pass. But da first sign I get dat he might fold, I'ma knock him down on B.J.," Shitty said dead serious talking about killing Sway.

"I feel you, but den we gonna have to kill Day-Day, Baby Boy, Eroc and Lips. And what if Sway won't even tell, you can't go off what you feel, bra," Squirt schooled trying to make Shitty see his point.

"Dat's law, bra, but I'm not taking any chances on whether a nigga might or might not tell on me. I already told Day-Day and Sway, Lips can't come around here anymore or it's gonna be a problem. But you gonna have to see what I'm talking 'bout," Shitty said.

"Yeah, burnt, bra! But I feel you a little bit," Squirt replied with a light laugh as he and Shitty quietly walked the rest of the way down Double R stuck in their own thoughts.

CHAPTER 24

"Y'all Day-Day ain't come back from round Edgewood yet?" Shitty yelled to his crew walking in the trap.

"Nah, dat nigga still ain't get here," Squirt replied, shaking his head looking at Shitty.

Shitty, Squirt, Sway and Lil' E was around the Yo in the trap waiting for Day-Day who was supposed to have been back an hour ago. Day-Day went around Edgewood to go grab two bulletproof vests he left over his aunt Wendy's house so they could go on a robbery they'd been planning for weeks.

"I'm tellin' y'all if dis nigga Day-Day ain't here in ten minutes, we gone," Shitty said mad Day-Day still ain't show up looking at his watch that read 9:15 p.m.

"Man, shut your cryin' ass up. Y'all ain't 'bout to pull another move without me," Day-Day said coming in the front door of the trap, smiling, with two bulletproof vests in his hand.

"Nah, for real. You smiling your ass was 'bout to get left," Shitty replied dead serious.

"Man, whatever, y'all ready or what?" Day-Day said throwing him a bulletproof vest.

"Yeah," Shitty said, catching the vest and putting it on over his Burberry hoody as he and the crew got off the couch and headed out the door to a stolen black on black four door Dodge Ram 1500.

Shitty being the best driver in their hood jumped in the driver's seat, while Day-Day jumped in the passenger seat and Lil' E, Squirt and Sway all got in the back. As they drove off heading to their move which was out Landover, Maryland in a hood called Kentland. Day-Day started asking Squirt more about the move since he was the one who brought it to the crew.

"So, Squirt, you say da nigga got at least ten pounds and fifty bands, right?" Day-Day asked looking at him through his rearview mirror.

"Bra, I told you like five times, he got at least dat. My cousin buys five pounds from da nigga a week and he be goin to his house to cop and say he don't ever have nothin' less than ten pounds," Squirt said with confidence, not knowing exactly what the dude they was going to rob really had.

"So, Squirt, didn't you say your cousin was over da nigga's house right now?" Shitty asked as he stopped at a red light.

"Yeah, he been waitin' on us. I'm goin' text him when we get out front da nigga house and he gonna leave out, and dat's gonna be our signal," Squirt said.

"Say less," Shitty said smiling.

That was the last words spoken between Shitty and his crew as he turned up *Yo' Gotti* featuring *YGN Lucci One on One* song that was playing in the truck as they headed to Landover.

❋ ❋ ❋ ❋ ❋ ❋

Less than twenty minutes later, Shitty and his crew were parking in the parking lot behind their vicks house.

"Text dat nigga!" Shitty yelled at Squirt as he parked and turned the car off.

"I'm already on it," Squirt replied texting his cousin.

As Squirt waited for his cousin to text back, Shitty and his crew made sure their guns was cocked and ready. Shitty had his Mac-10. Day-Day had a Glock 20. Lil' E and Sway both had Glock 27s, and Squirt had a Glock 30. Shitty and his crew had over 150 shots like they were going to a war rather than a robbery.

"Ay, look my cousin just text me back. He said it's only the two of dem niggas in dere. He comin' out now and gonna leave da door open for us," Squirt said to his whole crew.

"Bet," Day-Day said.

"Come on y'all, my cousin just left out," Squirt said, pointing at a tall, light-skinned dude with dreads walking and looking at his cell phone.

"Shid, we gone," Shitty said as he got out of the truck and everybody followed suit.

As they were walking to the front door of the vicks house they spotted two women, a baby and a man just talking outside chilling not paying them no mind. Shitty walked right through the front door, Mac in had without hesitation with his crew on his heels.

"Man, both of y'all get the fuck down!" Shitty yelled catching them off guard.

Squirt, Day-Day and Sway ran to check all the back rooms to make sure they were the only two there like Squirt's cousin said, while Lil' E stayed with him. Their two vicks was in the front room playing NBA 2k20 on playstation 4 and listening to rapper Lil Baby *Sumthin' 2 Prove*.

The main vick they came for was dark-skinned about 6'3, two-hundred pounds with a bald head. His partner was dark-skinned as well about 5'9, one-hundred and fifty pounds with shoulder length dreads in his hair. They both was so shocked that they just dropped their game controllers and stood up with their hands up.

"Didn't I say get da fuck down!" Shitty yelled, getting up on their main vick they came to rob and smacked him with his Mac-10 so hard he broke his nose.

"Ughhhh!" the dude yelled after getting smacked by Shitty with the Mac-10, feeling his nose break as he fell to the floor with blood squirting everywhere.

"What the fuck you waiting for? Get your bitch ass down!" Lil' E yelled, grabbing the other dude by the dreadlocks throwing him to the ground.

"Ay, Squirt, you ain't find nothing yet?" Day-Day yelled to the back of the house.

"Nah, I'm still lookin'," Squirt replied from the master bedroom.

Squirt, Day-Day and Sway was in all different rooms searching for drugs, money, jewelry or anything they felt was worth taking.

"Man, it got to be sumthin' in here," Squirt said talking to himself and checking under the bed.

"What the fuck is dis?" Squirt asked, grabbing a black and gray Armani Exchange bag.

"Oh, shit! Jackpot!" Squirt yelled excited when he opened the bag and saw what was inside.

Inside the bad was two bricks of coke, a scale and an all-black MP5 semi-automatic machine gun with a shoestring attached to it. Squirt closed the bag back and kept searching. He walked to the closet that was wide open, looked inside and saw a blue and red soccer duffle bag that was on the top shelf. Squirt tried to grab the duffle bag down so fast from the shelf that he slipped and fell over some New Balance shoe boxes that was on the closet floor.

"Fuckkk!" Squirt yelled, getting up from the floor.

"Man, what the fuck, you fell?" Day-Day asked, seeing Squirt getting up off the floor as he ran in the room with his Glock in hand ready to start shooting.

"What the fuck it looks like," Squirt replied off the floor.

"Grab dat soccer bag down," Squirt told Day-Day pointing to the duffle bag in the closet. Day-Day grabbed the bag down and opened it and looked inside.

"Moe, we gone!" Day-Day yelled to Squirt after seeing what was in the bag and closing it back.

He and Squirt left the bedroom, not noticing Squirt with the Armani Exchange bag in his hand. As they got back in the front room they saw that Shitty and Lil' E had stripped their two vicks ass naked. The two vicks was layin' on their stomachs with their hands behind their heads.

When Shitty saw them with the bags in their hands, he asked, "So, y'all ready?"

"Yeah, we got everything, we gone," Day-Day replied ready to leave.

"Where da fuck Sway at?" Lil E asked, looking toward the back.

"I'm right here," Sway said entering the front room.

"It wasn't shit in dere but dese two Rolexes," Sway said, holding up two gold Rolex watches.

"Dat shit ain't 'bout nothing, we cool," Squirt said excited knowing what he had in the Armani Exchange bag and the way that Day-Day acted when he opened the duffle bag that he must have come off good.

"We got to get the fuck now," Squirt continued walking toward the door.

"Hold up, dese niggas saw our faces. We got to kill dem," Day-Day said, looking at their two vicks.

"Dat's a no brainer!" Shitty yelled as he pointed his Mac-10 at their vicks and fired.

Blatt! Blatt! Blatt! Blatt! Blatt! Blatt! Blatt! Blatt!

Shitty fired spraying his Mac-10 filling their main vick's head and face up with bullets, then turning his Mac to their other vick. Before he even got the chance to aim his gun at the other vick Day-Day and Squirt beat him to the punch.

Boom! Boom! Boom! Boom! Boom! Boom! Bok! Bok! Bok!

They fired at the same time Day-Day was hitting their other vick 45 times with his 10. Millimeter in the back while Squirt gave him three 45 bullets to the back of his head.

"We gone," Sway said as he opened the front door and they all ran out headed to their truck at full speed.

As they were almost to their truck two P.G. County police officers pulled up and jumped out of their cars, gun drawn.

"Don't fuckin' move, or we will shoot y'all fuckin' heads off!" one of the white officer's yelled.

He and his partner pointed guns at Shitty and his crew, without a thought Sway, Day-Day and Lil E fired at the officers. They fired so many shots at once that the only thing the two officers could do was go for cover. As soon as Sway, Day-Day and Lil E started shooting at the police Shitty and Squirt took off running to their stolen truck and jumped in.

"Come on y'all!" Shitty yelled at the rest of his crew as he started the truck up.

As Sway, Day-Day and Lil E ran to their truck the police officers saw their chance to fire shots.

Pop! Pop! Pop! Pop! Pop! Pop!

One of the officers fired barely missing Sway being as though he was the last one to jump in the truck. As soon as they all made it in the truck, Shitty pulled off in reverse like he was starring in the movie *Too Fast Too Furious*.

"I'm 'bout to bust dey ass, kill," Shitty said, Shitty lived for high speed chases when he was younger and stealing cars. He used to pull up on police cruisers and throw eggs at them just so they could chase him, and to this day he never been caught behind the wheel.

"Watch out, bra!" Lil E yelled to Shitty.

It was another piece cruiser with a crash bar on the front of it that came out of nowhere trying to crash into their truck.

"Man, fall back and turn dat Moneybagg on, we good!" Shitty yelled to his little brother Lil' E as he swerved around the police car.

Squirt who was no in the passenger seat turned on Moneybagg Yo new CD *Time Served*, and as the *Me vs. Me* song blasted the speakers, Shitty with now two PG County State trooper police cruisers on him turned up behind the wheel. After about ten minutes of a couple of turns, back streets and going up the wrong sides of the streets. Shitty and his crew finally lost the police and was now at a red light on Benning Road Northeast by a seafood spot called *The Shrimp Boat*.

"Moe, you bust dey ass, bra, kill," Squirt said, smiling hard as shit and finally turned the music down.

"Kill!" Day-Day joined in.

"Y'all already know dem people can't fuck with me. But we got to get rid of dat hot ass truck," Shitty said as the light turned green for him to go.

Shitty headed back to their trap around the Yo to see what they hit for on the move.

* * * * * *

Back in their trap around the Yo', Shitty, and his crew was just finishing adding up what they had come off with from their move and was about to split it.

"Moe, we came off wit' twelve pounds of O.G, two keys of coke, thirty bands, two Rolies and a MP5," Squirt said to his crew looking at everything.

"Shid, I see what we came off with, let's split dat shit up," Lil E said geeking to get his cut. As they were trying to figure out how they were going to split up what they came off with from their move," Shitty said. "Ay, turn on da news and roll some of dat O.G. up. I know we made da motherfucker," Shitty said as Day-Day turned on the Fox 5 News and Sway started rolling up some backwoods of O.G.

As soon as Day-Day turned on the news they saw a breaking news story about a deadly shootout with PG County police out Landover, Maryland.

"I told y'all! We made dat motherfucker!" Shitty yelled amped up that they made the news.

"Turn dat shit up, Day-Day?" Squirt yelled, trying to hear exactly what they were saying.

Day-Day turned up the news just in time, the reporter was breaking the story...

"It has been a deadly shoot out here tonight in a neighborhood called Kentland here in Landover, Maryland. Two Prince George County police officers got into a big gun battle with five suspects as they were responding to a call of shots being fired from a house. The suspects fired over thirty shots at the officers after they were told to freeze, then jumped into a 2019 four door black Dodge Ram 1500 pick-up truck and sped off. Some of the shots fired at police by the suspects hit a mother and child who was just returning home, both are currently in stable condition and expected to recover.

"But if you'll look at the house behind me, that's currently roped off by detectives, it's the same house that the police officers were responding to after a call of shots being fired. They discovered a gruesome sight of two black males, dead, both in their late twenties. They were both riddled with bullets. One of the male victims was, Ricky Kelly, twenty-nine years old of Montgomery County, Maryland. The other victim was, twenty-six years old, Thomas Mill of Landover, Maryland. Right now, the Prince George County police department have very few leads, but if anyone has any leads please contact the..."

The news reporter was saying before Day-Day turned the TV off.

"Damn, Slim dat shit crazy. A lil' bitch and her baby got hit. If a nigga gets caught for dis dey gonna wash a nigga up, kill," Sway said putting his head down shaking it.

"Nah, for real," Lil E said, agreeing with Sway.

"Dat's cause y'all niggas need to learn how to shoot," Shitty said, laughing taking their current situation for a joke.

"Bra, you laughin'. But dis shit could get ugly fast," Squirt warned seriously thinking of the possibility of things going bad.

"Man, fuck all dat scared shit. What happened is already done, and what's gonna happen later we can't stop, so it is what it is," Shitty said looking at his whole crew.

"Moe, all y'all trippin'," Day-Day finally spoke up. "What Shitty said is law! We need to just split dis money and shit up and worry about that later, later." Day-Day continued splitting everybody's cut from the move up. "Look everybody gets six bands apiece. Shitty and Squirt said dey want da Rolies, so y'all don't get no O.G. and me, Lil E and Sway will get four pounds apiece. Day-Day said, looking at Shitty and Squirt.

"Bet!" Shitty said, looking at Squirt, smiling.

"A'ight, dat's a bet, and it's a one-thousand and eight grams in a brick. So, we get two-thousand and sixteen with both of dem. So, everybody gets four and two grams apiece give or take, and we take turns totin' da MP5," Squirt said being the cocaine master of the crew.

"Say less," Day-Day said, passing everybody six bands.

"Ay, ain't no scale in here. Flip took dat joint dis morning," Lil' E said to Squirt grabbing the MP5 putting it around his neck like a chain due to it having a shoestring attached on it.

161

RICO | KINGS OF THE YO

"Look, it's a scale still in dat bag. Y'all could go 'head and split dat shit up. I'll get my cut in the morning. I'm going in the house," Squirt said to his crew heading to the door.

"Bet," Day-Day said to Squirt grabbing the scale out the Armani Exchange bag and putting it on the table getting ready to weigh and split the coke up.

"Yeah, I'm goin', too. Lil E get my cut and I'll get it from you later. I told Mook I was goin' to be in da house three hours ago," Shitty said, following Squirt to the door.

"A'ight," Lil' E replied as Shitty and Squirt left out the front door heading in the house.

CHAPTER 25

"I told y'all dem da only two shooting and killing I know about!" Day-Day yelled to the two detectives getting mad.

Day-Day was down 36th and Minnesota in the back of a black unmarked police car with tinted windows talking to two homicide detectives. One short white one and the other fat and black. Day-Day got arrested two days after the big shootout. Day-Day was in his dark green Crown Victoria heading around the Yo after leaving his girl's house around 21st N.E. when he got pulled over by the D.C. Police and tried to run them, but crashed shortly after the chase and got caught. Day-Day got caught with Shitty's Mac-10, his own Glock 27, 2 ounces of heroin, 3 pounds of loud and $7300 in cash.

Day-Day knew Shitty Mac-10 probably had at least ten bodies on it. On top of the drugs and his Glock, he knew he was going to be locked up for at least twenty years with his criminal record. The only thing he could do to get out his current jam was snitch. As soon as he got to the homicide division in Southwest D.C., he told the homicide detectives he knew about a shootout, the murders out in Maryland, and another murder, and if they let him go he'd tell them

163

everything and they agreed. They were willing to take the shootings and murders over guns and drugs any day.

Day-Day told the two homicide detectives about the murder and shootout out Landover with the P.G. County police and about a murder him, Squirt and Shitty did a year ago around a hood called Lench Mob, but that wasn't even 10% of the murders he knew about. The detective gave Day-Day a week's free pass to call them at a good time when they could catch Shitty and his crew to lock them up on murder charges in D.C. and Maryland or he was going to jail for a long time.

Today was the last day of that week giving to him by the detectives and Day-Day kept his promise and called them. Day-Day told the detectives that he had just left Shitty and Squirt's and that they were still in the trap. He told them where it was and that they had the murder weapons for the crimes he'd told them about.

"All right, Mr. Tibbs. If we find out that you know about more murders and shit, you're going to fuck up a good deal for yourself," the short white detective said to Day-Day calling him by his last name with a serious look on his face.

"I already know da deal," Day-Day said shaking his head.

"Okay, Mr. Tibbs. You can go. I'ma call you later. I'ma go down to the precinct and see if I can get a warrant for Shitty, Squirt and the rest or your crew," the short white officer said looking at Day-Day.

"A'ight," Day-Day said before pulling the hood of his Hugo Boss hoodie on his head and getting out the unmarked police car. He then walked around the corner, got into his Crown Vic, and heading back around the Yo like nothing ever happened.

"That little motherfucker know more than what he is telling us!" the fat black detective said to his partner once Day-Day was out the car.

"Yeah, I know them little motherfuckers have beef with the whole city, but I got something for his little ass," the short, white detective replied to his partner. Turning on his car, he pulled off and headed back to the 1st district homicide division to try to get an arrest warrant.

* * * * * *

"Ay, Squirt! Where da fuck Day-Day say he was going, New York?" Shitty yelled coming down the steps being sarcastic as usual.

"He said he was going to holla at Mike down 34th to see if his mans wanna swap dem joints," Squirt replied.

"Damn, bra, dat nigga been gone for like two and a half hours, kill! Dat's like his third time since dat situation dat he disappeared like dat. He throwin' me off, real live," Shitty said as he sat down on the couch next to Squirt.

Just a week and a half ago Shitty, Squirt, Sway, Day-Day and Lil' E got into a big shootout with the P.G. County Police, after a robbery gone bad which left two men dead and two injured, including a woman and a child trying to get away from the crime scene. For the past two days they'd been hiding in the trap house due to the police playing their hood heavy and only going outside after the sun goes down to get something to eat.

"You make it seem like Day-Day hot or sumthin'! Tightin' up, bra, don't do dat," Squirt said firing up some O.G. dro they got off their last move.

"Man, whatever, bra. He ain't been disappearin' like dis and his brova Lips already hot. He still be fuckin' wit' him tough. Dat shit already been throwin' me off, kill. Like he condone dat shit! Told you Lil' E to leave da nigga around the Yo when we hit dat move out…" Shitty suddenly paused due to the loud knocks at the front door.

Boom! Boom! Boom! Boom! Boom!

"Open the fuckin' door, it's the police! Open the fuckin door!" they screamed.

As soon as the words police were screamed, Shitty and Squirt locked eyes.

"I told you, bra! I felt da shit! I should've smoked his lil' ass last night when I had da chance to, real live!" Shitty yelled, mad that he ain't follow his intentions like he always do.

"Man, you should've! Fuck dat shit now, we doing too much talkin'. We gotta get rid of dese guns! And fuck dem drugs, bra!" Squirt yelled as he grabbed his Glock 30 and Shitty's Mac-10 off the table.

The front door came crashing down…

To Be Continued…

COMING SOON!!!
Kings Of The Yo 2
Ain't No Picks

ABOUT THE AUTHOR

Rico is a 29 year old Washington, DC native and author. He is also the CEO of REAL SAVAGE PUBLICATIONS FOR BOOKS and MARI MURDA GANG FOR MUSIC. Rico is an original member of the GLIZZY GANG MUSIC GROUP that he and his childhood friends, including known rapper 'Shy Glizzy', started 2 years before his incarceration. He is currently locked up and has been since 2013. He is awaiting his release in 2022. If you want to know more about Rico, you can contact him using the information below.

Address:
Mauda'Rico Proctor 40790-007
FCI McDowell
P.O. Box 1009
Welch, WVA 24801

Instagram:
KingReek_MMG
RICGLIZZY_37

Real Savage Publications and TMC Presents...

The Real Shropshire Organization:
The Un-told Truth Behind
The Alleged Heroin Organization Protected
By Baltimore Police Detectives.

By Antonio "Brill" Shropshire

COMING SOON!!!

www.ingramcontent.com/pod-product-compliance
Lightning Source LLC
Chambersburg PA
CBHW072012290326
41934CB00007BA/1062